Connie

GOD'S DOORKEEPERS

Padre Pio, Solanus Casey and André Bessette

JOEL R. SCHORN

franciscan
media
Cincinnati, Ohio

Cover design by Candle Light Studios
Cover photo by Daniel Wildman Photography
Book design by Phillips Robinette, O.F.M.

LIBRARY OF CONGRESS CATALOGING-IN-PUBLICATION DATA

Schorn, Joel.
  God's doorkeepers : Padre Pio, Solanus Casey and Andre Bessette / Joel R. Schorn.
    p. cm.
  Includes bibliographical references (p.   ) and index.
  ISBN-13: 978-0-86716-699-6 (pbk. : alk. paper)
  ISBN-10: 0-86716-699-1 (pbk. : alk. paper) 1. Catholics—Biography. 2. Pio, of Pietrelcina, Saint, 1887-1968. 3. Andre, Brother, 1845-1937. 4. Casey, Solanus, 1870-1957. I. Title.

BX4669.S36 2006
282.092'2—dc22
[B]
2006016893

ISBN 978-0-86716-699-6

Published by Franciscan Media
28 W. Liberty St.
Cincinnati, OH 45202
www.FranciscanMedia.org

22 21 20 19 18 9 8 7 6 5

Contents

Part Three: HOLY WORKS

Part Four: HOLY LIVES

Acknowledgments

"Thank God ahead of time," Solanus used to say, and so I will.

My loudest thanks go to my wife, Edwina, for her support during the research and writing of this book, which included accompanying me on a drive through a Detroit snowstorm to visit the Solanus Casey Center.

And I must express my gratitude to editor Cynthia Cavnar and the rest of the staff of Servant Books and St. Anthony Messenger Press for their enthusiasm and work in connection with this book.

Thanks also to those who taught me about the door-keepers and in one way or another encouraged me to write about them, especially Father Michael Crosby, Father André Léveillé, Joseph Durepos, Jim Manney, Margadette Demet and the people of the Padre Pio prayer group of the Shrine of Our Lady of Pompeii in Chicago.

An "acknowledgment" must also go to the door-keepers themselves, Brother André, Father Solanus and Padre Pio. I have learned not only of their remarkable lives but also of the continuing power of their inter-cessory prayer.

Solanus, André and Pio built up networks of friends that continue today: those who worked with them, knew them for many years, came to them for help or simply prayed through their intercession. They had close, personal friends, and Padre Pio adopted some as his spiritual daughters and sons to carry out his mission in a special way. But everyone who came to them, whether in person or through prayer—and the latter group includes all who have come to them in prayer since their deaths—came as a friend.

The doorkeepers have become my friends as well. They have helped to show me what love is—for God, for Christ and his holy church, for goodness and for the presence of Christ in those around me.

Introduction

*Every era has to produce its saints, just as every year
has to produce its own wheat.*

—Madame Katharina Tangari, *Stories of Padre Pio*

No one should have heard of André Bessette (1845–1937), Solanus Casey (1870–1957) and Padre Pio (1887–1968). Had their lives been "normal," it's likely they would have passed their time tucked away in houses of their religious orders, quietly performing their duties.

Their beginnings were not promising. André came from a poor background. With almost no education, he wanted to join the Congregation of Holy Cross as a working brother, which back then meant he would do mostly menial tasks. He was prone to illness, and at first the community did not want to be burdened with such a sickly and unpromising individual. After an intervention by the archbishop of Montréal, however, the community let André in and made him a porter, or doorkeeper.

A bright youth but a mediocre student, Francis Casey had to leave the diocesan seminary. Moving on to the Capuchin Franciscan order, he barely made it through his training. His community allowed him to be ordained but with conditions: Father Solanus could say Mass but not preach or hear confessions. Almost everywhere he lived, his superiors assigned him to be the community's porter, a position in which he dealt with visitors to the monastery.

Pio grew up in very humble circumstances in the Italian town of Pietrelcina. After a spiritually unusual childhood, during which he experienced mystical visions even at a young age, this devout young man entered the Capuchins. He suffered illnesses and moved from monastery to monastery, eventually ending up in the remote Italian mountain town of San Giovanni Rotondo. While Pio was not literally a doorkeeper, he shares with Brother André and Father Solanus the vocation of guiding people through the doorways of holiness.

Despite their humble exteriors, God chose these men to serve the poor and suffering. They were signs of God's loving presence, spending hours listening to afflicted people and praying for them. Through them flowed miraculous gifts of healing, love and compassion and works of mercy.

Sometimes Father Solanus knew his visitors' problems before they even said anything. Blessed André prayed for people and anointed the sick with oils blessed through prayers to Saint Joseph. Many experienced healing; others were encouraged and comforted. When Father Solanus died, twenty thousand people came to his wake. Brother André's funeral brought an estimated one million mourners.

While André and Solanus stood at the doors of their monasteries, Padre Pio opened the doors of the confessional to literally thousands. There and in other encounters he led people to healing relationships with God. His extraordinary supernatural gifts attracted a worldwide following. A hundred thousand people attended his funeral, and today Pio's monastery in San Giovanni Rotondo is the second most visited Catholic shrine in the world. It is also home to a modern hospital Pio established.

I think there is a connection between the lowliness of André, Solanus and Pio and their tremendous gifts of healing and compassion. What they did grew out of who they were. God drew near to them because they drew near to God.

Obedience

True humility and obedience have to do with putting others—God and people—ahead of oneself. André, Solanus and Pio almost perfectly embodied this humility. Near the end of his life, Solanus Casey said, "I look on my whole life as giving, and I want to give and give until there is nothing left of me to give."[1] These words could as well come from the mouth of Brother André or Padre Pio.

Their humility showed in their sense of obedience. Their most immediate schools of obedience were in the religious orders of their day, where the will of a superior was the will of God. "If my superiors ordered me to jump out of the window, I would not argue. I would jump," Padre Pio said.[2]

It was the same for Brother André. During some early opposition to his healing ministry, his superiors considered transferring him to New Brunswick. He would have gone, he said, because it would have been the will of God.

Capuchin Brother Ignatius Milne said of Solanus: "I think Father Solanus was imbued with the spirit of obedience. I never found him to criticize or complain or object to the will of his superior, whether it was fair or unjust. His attitude was that this is the will of God and if it is meant to be different in time, it will work out."[3] The order gave Solanus short notice of moves throughout his life as a Capuchin, sometimes to his surprise. One of his transfers allowed him only twenty-four hours to get to his new assignment.

Obedience was for these men part of a much larger attitude. At its root obedience means *listening:* listening to the will of God and to how God is working in the lives of people. In this sense the doorkeepers had their ears constantly attuned to the voice of God. "Trust God," Brother André said. "He is very close to you; He listens to you."[4]

The holiness of Solanus, André and Pio came from their prayerfulness, their patience, their total desire to trust God's will and do it. We see in them the power of prayer, of the nearly infinite depth of patience if we call on it, of the freedom of seeing God in everything that happens to us, good or bad, and of giving up our desire to control, accepting life as it comes and submitting to the ways of God.

Miracles

Thousands of miracles attest to the fact that these men were wonder-workers of the first order. Many people react to such miracles by saying there is no rational explanation for them; they happen because God decided to suspend natural laws in particular cases. A doctor said of an early healing connected to Brother André, "A supernatural intervention, a miracle, is the only logical and intelligent explanation of a healing of which the reality alone, not the extraordinary character, could be doubted."[5]

Even for the skeptical the sheer number of stories makes it impossible to explain the miracles as wishful thinking, delusion or natural phenomena. In fact, a truly rational person would look at the evidence and have to conclude that something supernatural was going on.

John McCaffery, a spiritual son of Padre Pio, wrote of the padre, "Thousands of rational, cold-thinking people will testify that he is not only the holiest man they have ever met but that he has been the channel of innumerable preternatural manifestations in their regard."[6] "The logical deduction" that one doctor came to concerning the padre's stigmata could describe all the wonders God worked through the doorkeepers: "There was only one possible explanation, that of benign superhuman intervention."[7]

Yet for these men the extraordinary occurrences their prayer brought about have a meaning beyond the spectacular. God's action is the reason behind a miracle, so every miracle involves *faith*. "Where there is real faith and *confidence* in God there is no such thing as a hopeless case,"[8] Solanus once wrote.

And André, Solanus and Pio were people of faith. They had an almost total focus on God. And they brought people to faith; that was the ultimate purpose of the healings. One of Brother André's closest friends, Joseph Pichette, said, "I was under the impression that he healed the bodies in order to get to the souls."[9]

In other words, healing resulted from people's faith and also led them to faith. Carlo Campanini, the Italian comic and friend of Padre Pio, had been listening to story after story of miraculous cures brought about through the prayers of Padre Pio when he exclaimed, "All terrific! All fantastic! But remember that neither of you had a cure like mine." To one who questioned him on this he explained, "You, my friend, were cured of cancer of the throat. Absolute child's play! I was healed of cancer of the soul. That, believe me, is a miracle much more difficult to achieve."[10]

People to Follow

The doorkeepers offer us examples to imitate: Because they so closely imitated Christ, in following them we draw close to the Lord. The church recognizes this: She has declared Padre Pio a saint—Saint Pio of Pietrelcina—and has beatified Brother André, one step short of canonization. Solanus Casey's cause for canonization is progressing rapidly.

Above all, the doorkeepers show us how faith, closeness to God and seeking God in all things are the keys that unlock our lives. These men teach us to be open to God and other people. They demonstrate how absolute trust in and thankfulness to God can see us through anything. They witness to the goodness and spiritual power that grow out of choosing the vocation of humility. They empower us to live out our faith in giving ourselves in the patient service of others. They help us to see that the healing path leads through suffering and not around it. And in all this they lead us to joy.

Even as children and deeply devoted youths, Solanus, André and Pio cleaved to faith. They found their deepest happiness in a life of faith, in prayer and in the church. For them "the faith" was everything—both believing in God and in Catholic tradition. Perhaps the greatest gift they have to give is their testimony to the power of faith.

God waits patiently for us, just as Solanus and André waited at their porter stations and Pio waited in the confessional or the monastery garden. We are all afflicted in some way and to some degree. If we only turn to God, God will turn to us in a healing way.

"Follow the saints," said the first-century bishop Clement of Rome, "because those who follow them will become saints."[11] Solanus, André and Pio are saints of God who open the doors to God's presence. In walking through those doors, we can find healing and perhaps even can become saints ourselves.

PART ONE
BEGINNINGS

CHAPTER ONE

A Working Brother

I'm sending you a saint.

—Father André Provençal

Alfred Bessette was born in a one-room cabin on August 9, 1845, in the Québec town of Saint Grégoire d'Iberville. He was the sixth of ten children. Because he nearly died at birth, his parents gave him an emergency baptism at home. The next day his family celebrated a formal baptism at the local building that served as both parish church and town hall.

The family was poor, hardworking and devout. Isaac Bessette eked out a living for the family as a carpenter, not being able to get much from farming the long, narrow piece of land he owned behind the cabin.

Alfred's mother, the former Clothilde Foisy, counted two distant cousins among the church's honorees: Blessed Marie-Rose Durocher, the nineteenth-century Sister of the Holy Names of Jesus and Mary who taught in French Canada, and Saint Margaret d'Youville, who founded the Sisters of Charity "Grey Nuns" in eighteenth-century Montréal.

Alfred's relationship with his mother did much to form him. According to a friend, "Brother André always had a deep devotion to Saint Joseph, an inclination he owed to his mother,"[1] who also gave him his devotion to the Blessed Virgin Mary. Because he was the sickliest of the ten Bessette children who survived childhood, André said his mother showed "more love and care for me than for the others."[2]

When Alfred was ten years old, his father was out cutting wood with Alfred's older brother Isaïe. A tree came down the wrong way and, as Brother André expressed it years later, "crushed my poor father to instantaneous death."[3] Isaïe Bessette could not speak for days after his father's death, and Clothilde, who apparently was already suffering from tuberculosis, went into a slow decline.

Isaac Bessette left behind ten mouths to feed and an increasingly sick widow. The children who were old enough went to work. Alfred, age eleven, did not have the money for the fee to be apprenticed to a tradesman, so he did manual labor on nearby farms. Because no public school system existed at the time, and his family could not even come close to affording a private education for the children, Alfred simply did not go to school during the time he lived at home.

In November of 1857 Clothilde Bessette died at the age of forty-three. On her deathbed she told her children, "Believe in God. Never abandon your faith. Never fail to go to Mass on Sundays."[4]

Clothilde's death forced the members of the family to either go out on their own or live with relatives. Alfred went to stay with his mother's sister Rosalie Nadeau and her husband and children in the nearby town of St-Césaire. He was forever grateful to his aunt and uncle, who were shopkeepers, for sending him to school, if only briefly. After Alfred received his First Communion a few months later, he left school for good and became an apprentice to a shoemaker.

Ill health—especially digestive problems—was Alfred's almost constant companion. His first job did not help. "Working at shoemaking," André said later, "almost on all fours, striking the hammer all day, is not good for the digestion."[5] He also suffered from headaches.

When his uncle left for California to prospect for gold, Alfred became an itinerant laborer, working as an assistant baker, blacksmith, wood-hauler and construction worker. He eventually returned to St-Césaire to work once again as a farmhand. Though small and ill, manual labor made him "strong as an ox."[6] He retained this strength into later life, sometimes surprising those who did not expect much from his five-foot-three, 110-pound frame.

Also strong were his faith and devotion. A family he lived with at the time described him as "a very sickly young man. He could digest practically nothing. He rarely went out. But he was very kind, and he was always praying."[7] "Nobody could be any more pious!" an employer said of him. He sang hymns while he worked and prayed as much as he could. His sister Alphonsine reported, "Alfred was a good boy and an excellent young man. He was very pious. He took communion often. He spent all Sunday in church."[8] Alfred evangelized his friends. He told them stories from the Bible and exhorted them to live faithful and good lives. His devotion to and trust in Saint Joseph earned him the nickname "Saint Joseph's fool."[9] "Pray to Saint Joseph!" he would tell his friends. "He will not fail to obtain all your requests!"[10]

The American Civil War created jobs for Canadians who were willing to make the trip south to work in war industries. Many of Alfred's siblings ended up relocating to New England, and Alfred followed them, taking the train from Iberville to Nashua, New Hampshire. After a time he joined four of his sisters and brothers working in a Connecticut cotton mill. To counteract the dangerous and unhealthy environment of the mills, Alfred wisely alternated factory work and farm work.

In 1867 he decided to return to Canada. His first destination was Sutton, Québec, where two of his siblings were living. There he kept the grounds for the parish priest. When this priest was transferred, Alfred went back to St-Césaire and his former farmhand job. He lived with his aunt and uncle. The village was also the home of a longtime acquaintance, Father André Provençal.

Vocation
The farmer he worked for, Louis Ouimet, noticed that Alfred did not come back right away from the barn when he went to tend the horses. Finally Louis went to see what was going on. Alfred "had placed a cross in the back of the barn. He was on his knees, praying. That happened many times. When I realized he was like that,

I spoke of it to [Father] Provençal, who told me, 'Bring him to me.'"[11]

Religious life seemed the natural vocation for Alfred. He told Father Provençal, "I want to enter religion to serve the good God and sanctify myself. I want to be able to pray more easily. It is only among the priests at church and at devotions that I feel happy."[12]

While Alfred lacked the education to become a priest, becoming a working brother was a possibility. Provençal thought of Montréal's College of Notre-Dame, which the Congregation of Holy Cross operated. Father Provençal wrote a letter of recommendation to the college and, with the young man's devotion in mind, included the line: "I'm sending you a saint."[13]

The Congregation of Holy Cross was only eight years older than Alfred. Its founder, the French priest Basile Moreau, still had three years to live when Alfred presented himself to Holy Cross. The order's name came from the town of Ste-Croix, near Le Mans in northwestern France. There Moreau had merged two existing communities, the Brothers of Saint Joseph, who taught rural children, and the Auxiliary Priests of Le Mans, a kind of mission band that preached and gave retreats in the diocese. Moreau also founded a women's branch of the order, the Sisters of Holy Cross.

The men's order was made up of priests, educated teaching brothers, who ran the order's schools, and working brothers, who did the menial tasks necessary for the community. The working brothers received separate formation, much of which consisted of memorization because many of these young men were illiterate or only marginally literate. Ironically, this rote training served André well throughout his life. By reading and rereading, he memorized major portions of the Bible and other religious works.

Holy Cross came to Canada in 1847 at the request of the archbishop of Montréal, Ignace Bourget, who needed teaching brothers to staff the schools he was developing. Moreau, wanting to keep together the order he had assembled from different communities, insisted the bishop accept priests, sisters and brothers or get nothing at all. Bourget agreed to this arrangement, and by 1870 Holy Cross operated a high school in St-Laurent and primary schools in St-Césaire and Côtes-des-Neiges, between Montréal and St-Laurent.

The twenty-five-year-old Alfred became a candidate for membership in Holy Cross in November 1870 and a month later became a novice. Holy Cross priests could keep their given names, but brothers took a new name. During the liturgy of reception into the novitiate, Alfred heard the words, "Your name in the world was Alfred Bessette. Henceforth you will have the name Brother André." Whether he chose the name or his superiors gave it to him, the inspiration came from the man who had steered him to Holy Cross, his friend Father André Provençal.

A Fortunate Intervention

André was happy in his new life as a novice. Beyond his piety, however, what did he have to offer Holy Cross, or any religious community for that matter? He could not read very well, could barely write and seemed to be chronically ill. Severe stomach cramps confined him to bed for days at a time.

Though the community admitted him as a novice, the task it assigned him reflected his lack of promise: He became the janitor. The tasks, though hard, were less physically demanding than the heavy manual labor expected of working brothers. In effect, André became the lowest of the low, a novice working brother below the other working brothers.

After a year André's superiors barred him from taking the next step in joining the community. "Brother André is not permitted to take his temporary vows because his health does not allow us to think he will ever be admitted to the [Perpetual] Profession."[14] A working brother was supposed to work, and if he couldn't work, he would be nothing but a burden.

Usually such a development meant the end of the line for a novice. In Alfred's case it probably would have cast him back into the precarious life of a wandering laborer. But he was determined, perhaps desperate at the thought of being cut off from the only life in which he felt he could be happy. So he took a bold step.

Shortly after the negative decision on André's future, Archbishop Bourget of Montréal made a visit to the school where André was serving. André approached him and told him of the situation. "I knelt before him," Brother André said, "with my clasped hands on his knee. [Monsignor] Bourget spoke to me like a father."[15] In an intervention for which the whole church can be grateful, the archbishop told André, "The community will keep you."[16]

The governing council of the province, in admitting André to temporary and finally perpetual vows, noted, "All members of the Council are agreed to approve Brother André's admission to the religious profession, whilst remarking that though his health is rather weak, the Brother nevertheless remains quite capable of rendering fine services to the Congregation in view of his zeal and piety." The master of novices said of him, "If this young man becomes unable to work, he will at least know how to pray."[17]

At the Door

After André took his vows as a brother, Holy Cross assigned him to the boys' school, or "college," it ran in Montréal, Notre-Dame-des-Neiges, "Our Lady of the Snows." At the time of André's arrival at the school, the Côtes-des-Neiges ("Hill of Snow") area outside of Montréal was more or less out in the country. Because his superiors did not think him up to the task of laboring on the community's farm, they made him porter, or doorkeeper, one of the lowest positions in the community.

Years later André joked, "My superiors showed me the door and I stayed there," and, "I was at the door forty years without going out."[18] According to the Holy Cross constitutions of the time, the porter lived, ate and prayed somewhat separately from the community, near the entrance. Brother André's first room had a roughly upholstered bench for a bed, a wardrobe, a pitcher and a bowl. Only a crucifix and an image of Saint Joseph hung on the walls.

The tasks of the porter involved answering the door, finding persons whom visitors came to see, keeping track of visitors, signing the students in and out, delivering packages and mail and greeting and preparing a meal for members of the community when they returned from trips. Brother André also met homeless people who came to the door, getting them something to eat and treating them with great respect. He picked up students' clothes from their homes each week, awakened the community every morning, helped the young children in the bathroom, cut hair, sewed, fixed things, took care of the wine cellar, swept, cleaned the outhouses, mended shoes, gardened, watched for fires and burglars and cleaned the windows.

From time to time it was André's responsibility to care for patients in the infirmary (a task that would later occasion some healings). He also prepared for burial the bodies of community members who had died as well as the bodies of those in the surrounding area who could not afford an undertaker—a task that disturbed him. "Nights after he laid out bodies of the dead, Brother André had difficulty sleeping and heard frightening noises in his room."[19]

Speaking later in life of all his responsibilities, Brother André said, "I never refused to do what was asked of me. I always answered, 'Yes,' and I finished at night what I couldn't do in the day." Many nights he got little sleep but still rose early in the morning to start his round of work all over again. In light of all these jobs, Brother André once said, "A good-for-nothing is good for everything."[20]

Thus André passed much of the early years of his vocation in the quiet and relentless work of porter. During this period he also gained the affection of those who knew him, especially the students and their parents. Because he was kind and listened to their problems, the boys loved him. He taught them prayers, talked to them about Saint Joseph and exhorted them to be more faithful. Some of the students he knew became priests in the United States and played host to Brother André when he traveled there years later.

"For us," one of his students noted, "Brother André was perfection. We respected him, we greeted him, and he always had a beautiful smile."[21] André earned a similar reputation with the boys' parents. When he ran errands to their homes, he often ended up listening to their troubles. And the Holy Cross brothers and priests believed Brother André's holiness, devotion and prayer protected the Notre-Dame-des-Neiges community from harm.[22]

But his heavy round of regular tasks took a toll on him. He contracted pneumonia and began to spit blood. Ordered to rest completely for two months, André said to his formidable and short-tempered superior at that time, Father Augustin Louage, "Would it bother you if I died quietly here at the house, or while washing windows? If it doesn't make any difference to you, it doesn't make any difference to me." Finding him at work again, his doctor warned him he could die if he continued. "If I die," Brother André replied, "the community will well be rid of me!"[23]

His digestive problems also continued to plague him. The exact nature of this condition is not known; he almost never saw a doctor or sought healing for himself. For most of his life, though, he endured "headache, intestinal cramps, stomach pains, heartburn, constipation, and assorted other digestive ills."[24]

His weak stomach did not allow him to eat much. His breakfast was coffee and a piece of bread. In the evening he ate what various witnesses described as bread crumbled in warm milk, water and milk boiled together or "little balls of flour which he cooked in bouillon or even water."[25] When he traveled and stayed with others, he ate sparingly whatever was put in front of him, even if he did not like it.

André seems to have had a purpose beyond the avoidance of indigestion. He ascribed to what he saw as a healthy program of "eat as little as possible and work as much as possible."[26]

André labored almost his whole life up to twenty hours a day and lived into his nineties. "Brother André was a frail man," a contemporary Holy Cross religious has written, "but he also showed an extraordinary vitality."[27]

CHAPTER TWO

"Go to Detroit"

*Considering the lack of my talents, I leave it to
my superiors to judge on my faculties and
to dispose of me as they think best.*

—Solanus Casey

Bernard Francis (Barney) Casey was born November
25, 1870, in a log cabin on a farm near Prescott,
Wisconsin, on the banks of the Mississippi River. He
was the sixth of ten boys and six girls, the children of
Bernard James Casey and Ellen Elizabeth Murphy.

Barney's Irish roots went deep, and he had an intense
lifelong interest in Irish affairs. His maternal grandfather had died in the potato famine around 1847, while
some said his paternal grandfather, James Casey, died
defending the parish church from a group of Protestant
raiders. Solanus believed his Grandfather James to be
a martyr.

Having sailed separately for the United States,
Bernard Sr. and Ellen Murphy met through Bernard's
sister at a Fourth of July picnic at Biddeford, Maine,

in 1860. Bernard was working as a shoemaker near Danvers, Massachusetts, while Ellen labored at a textile mill in the Portland, Maine, area. The relationship developed quickly, but Ellen was only sixteen, and her mother told the couple they had to wait three years before they could get married.

As if to reinforce the separation, Ellen's mother took her to Hastings, Minnesota, home of a married daughter who was expecting a child. Ellen found a job in St. Paul with Ignatius Donnelly, a writer, lecturer and later United States senator.

Back in Massachusetts Bernard tried to keep in touch with Ellen but found it difficult. Eventually he called upon his pastor to correspond with Ellen's pastor and so keep the lines of communication open. When the Donnellys made a trip to Washington, D.C., Ellen came with them and was reunited with Bernard. The two married on October 6, 1863, in Salem, Massachusetts. Their first child, also named Ellen, was born in July of 1864. James, their second child, was born the following year.

Farm Life

In the meantime, Owen and Patrick Murphy, Ellen's brothers, moved to Wisconsin to homestead. When the shoe business played out, Bernard and Ellen decided to follow them. They bought eighty acres of land near Prescott, overlooking the Mississippi River and adjoining the property of the Murphy brothers.

In the next five years Ellen and Bernard had four more children, including the boy who received his father's name. Barney's first memories included the sound of the Mississippi River flowing below the bluff and the sight of his mother hanging laundry in the yard, from which she could call to her neighbor across the river.

After the birth of another son, and with a new baby on the way, in 1873 Bernard Sr. bought a larger farm to the east on the Trimbelle River and moved his family there. Years later Solanus estimated the new house to be about twelve feet by seventy feet. On the ground floor a divider separated the girls' bedroom from that of the parents, while the boys slept in a loft.

A terrible blow struck the Caseys in 1878 when black diphtheria took the lives of Mary, age twelve, and three days later Martha, three. Some of the brothers, including Barney, also became sick, but they survived. The disease left Barney's voice thin and high-pitched.

In 1882 the Caseys moved again, with a new baby girl in tow, to a larger and better-equipped farm, a 345-acre place to the north in St. Croix County, near Burkhardt, Wisconsin. It had a large house, several farm buildings, a lake, the nearby Willow River and a railroad line that stopped two miles from the house.

In the slow winter months Bernard Sr. sold religious books and subscriptions to the *Irish Standard* and *Extension* magazines. He would pick up the materials in St. Paul, then ride the train back home. As the train passed through the farm, Bernard would throw the books and magazines out the window. His boys would pick them up, then Bernard would get off the train in Burkhardt and walk home.

The family was close-knit and devout. At seven o'clock every evening, Bernard Sr. rang a bell to gather the children to pray the rosary. To the male children doing outside chores he called, "Prayer, boys, prayer!"[1]

Typical of devout Catholic farm families of the era, the Caseys prayed before and after just about everything—in the morning, at meals and in the evening—for what they needed to survive and for safety from the disasters of farm life, like bad weather, fires and diseases of the crops and livestock. Frequent family rosaries were part of Barney's life.

The family attended church regularly, but the remoteness of the farm called for some improvisation. The Caseys owned only one wagon and could not fit everyone in it, so half of the family went to church one Sunday and the other half the next. The half left at home read the Mass prayers together. "Sometimes," Solanus recalled to his sister in 1930, those prayers "seemed pretty long."[2]

Barney's education probably started in the home, and when he entered the Burkhardt schools, he did well. The debate team he led won several prizes, and he took to literature and poetry, to which his parents had first exposed him and his siblings.

Stepping Out

After poor harvests in the mid-1880s, Barney journeyed to Stillwater, twenty miles away, across the St. Croix River in Minnesota, for his first job off the farm. He helped move logs down the St. Croix for one of Stillwater's logging operations. This work was seasonal. When winter came the river froze, leaving huge frozen logjams until the spring's thaw.

Barney then obtained a job as a handyman and substitute guard in the state prison, where his uncle Pat Murphy was a guard. It was a sign of Barney's personableness that Cole Younger, who was a member of the infamous James Younger gang, gave him a wooden chest, which he kept for many years.[3] Barney also worked for a while at a brick kiln.

In Stillwater Barney lived with his Uncle Pat and Aunt Mary. When a visitor left a violin, he took it up. He eventually became good enough to play at local dances, though his siblings required that at home he practice in the barn (a resistance to his playing that his brother Capuchins shared in future years!).

He also became interested in a young woman, Rebecca Tobin, who lived on a farm neighboring the Caseys. They saw quite a bit of each other, and the relationship developed to the point where Barney proposed marriage. Rebecca's mother, however, thought her too young to marry and sent her to a girls' school in St. Paul. Barney never saw her again, nor did he enter into another serious relationship with a woman. Sometime later he found out that she had died at a relatively young age.

Stillwater was one of the first towns in the Midwest to build an electric streetcar system, and Barney began working as a conductor. When the prospect of a better streetcar job opened in the town of Appleton, he moved there. He supplemented his income by coloring photographs. (The present-day Solanus Casey Center in Detroit has a photo from Solanus's Capuchin life that he tinted, drawing on his skills from his days in Appleton.)

Barney worked in Appleton for about a year before getting another streetcar job in the northern Wisconsin city of Superior, a boomtown near which some of his brothers already owned some land. He did well in these jobs, started training other men and eventually became a motorman in Superior.

Back home the family farm had suffered a run of three bad years, and Barney encouraged the rest of the family to move to Superior. His father sold the farm and bought land next, to add to the forty acres his three oldest sons owned. On the new property a ten-room house accommodated the Caseys.

God's Call

Barney's brother Maurice had already begun studies for the priesthood when Barney "began to wonder if possibly there couldn't be two priests in a family."[4] The thought of becoming a priest had occurred to him when he was quite young, before his First Communion, while attending midnight Mass. Eventually the family would see three sons enter the priesthood: Barney, Maurice and Edward.

While contemplating the possibility of priesthood, Barney had an experience that had a decisive impact on him. One day the streetcar came to a halt for a woman lying on the tracks bleeding, while an intoxicated sailor threatened her with a knife. Versions of this story differ, and it's unclear whether the man actually killed the woman. But the devout Barney prayed for both the victim and her attacker, and in this prayer he started thinking that he wanted to help alleviate all the world's suffering.

He went to see the saintly Eustace Vollmer, a Franciscan priest in Superior who directed the Third Order Franciscans, to which both Barney's parents belonged. Father Vollmer suggested that Barney talk with his pastor, Father Edmund Sturm of Sacred Heart parish. Father Sturm recommended that Barney attend the St. Francis de Sales Diocesan Seminary in Milwaukee.

Barney faced several handicaps on entering the seminary. First was his age. Because he had only a primary education, at age twenty-one he had to attend the seminary high school with boys a few years younger.

Second was language. St. Francis de Sales Seminary was at the heart of Midwestern German-American Catholicism, Milwaukee forming the German-American "triangle" with St. Louis and Cincinnati. Of the thirteen professors who taught there when Barney arrived, only two spoke English. Textbooks were in Latin, and classes were in German, languages of which he had no prior knowledge.

The third obstacle was Barney's lack of experience as a student. While he had finished eighth grade, his need to work both on the family farm and at paying jobs took him away from a focus on schoolwork that would have prepared him for the demands of seminary studies. From everything we know of Solanus, he was quick-minded and bright. His intelligence, however, was highly intuitive, and he had difficulty applying himself to studies. As he put it, his "brain just didn't seem to want to work."[5]

Then there was his health. An aftereffect of his childhood bout with diphtheria was unusually frequent peritonsillar infections, which swelled his throat and produced fevers and sharp pain.

On top of these factors, Barney needed to earn money to help pay his tuition, which took time and energy away from his studies. He became the seminary barber, mirroring the work of Brother André, who cut hair to pick up money for the first Oratory of St. Joseph. When the seminary started a dairy farm, Barney put his rural upbringing to work and helped with the chores.

His good nature and his experience with younger brothers helped him overcome the age difference between him and the other students, and he was well-liked. In fact, he became something of a surrogate older brother to the others, resolving quarrels among them. He anchored baseball games, reprising his role from the "Casey Nine"—the baseball team made up of Casey boys—of the fearless catcher who played without a mask.

The language and academic obstacles, however, proved harder to overcome. Barney went through the four years of high school seminary and the first semester of his college-level education with good marks for his "academics, application, and conduct," the three areas in which seminarians received grades.[6] At this point, however, his grades began to decline, to the point where his superiors informed him that they did not think he had the academic ability to continue. Though Barney had worked hard, his inexperience as a student caught up with him, as did the conditions he faced at the diocesan seminary.

The seminary rectors did not leave him out in the cold. They directed him to the Capuchin Franciscans in downtown Milwaukee. Perhaps his vocation would find a home there.

The Capuchins

Barney's visit to the Capuchin seminary, also named for Saint Francis, did not encourage him. He once

again found the curriculum in Latin and the teaching
in German. On top of that, this particular Capuchin
province, that of St. Joseph, was known for the austerity
of its lifestyle. Like Padre Pio, Barney was looking at
one of the stricter communities of what was in general
a strict order. The Capuchins' untrimmed beards also
put him off!

During the summer of 1896, home in Superior once
again, Barney had some discerning to do. Having failed
at the diocesan seminary and now considering joining a
religious order, the whole question of whether he was
going to be a priest hung in the balance. He spoke again
to Father Vollmer, who affirmed Barney's vocation to
religious life and the priesthood and recommended
that he apply to the Franciscans—Father Vollmer's
own community of Friars Minor—the Jesuits and the
Capuchins.

Barney also prayed. In particular, he drew on his
devotion to the Blessed Virgin Mary. Back in Stillwater
he had nearly died trying to save a drowning man, only
to feel himself pulled up when he grabbed the scapular
of Our Lady of Mount Carmel his mother had given
him. Now, facing a decision about where to pursue the
priesthood, he asked his mother and sister to join him
in a novena coinciding with the Solemnity of the
Immaculate Conception of the Blessed Virgin Mary.

At the end of the novena, Barney made a spontaneous personal vow of chastity, and immediately the
words "Go to Detroit" entered his consciousness. He
knew what they meant. The novitiate of the Capuchin
Province of St. Joseph was in Detroit. Therefore, if they
would have him, he would join the Capuchins. He was

convinced the message was a favor of Our Lady and a sign from God.

Barney soon received the go-ahead from the Capuchins. The provincial wrote, "You may...come to Detroit, as soon as circumstances will allow you, or the sooner the better for yourself."[7]

So he began an early winter train journey, first from St. Paul to Milwaukee, where he spent the night, then to Chicago, where he changed trains for the final leg to Detroit. In the midst of a snowstorm, the train averaged twelve miles per hour. It arrived in Detroit as the sun went down on Christmas Eve 1896.

Barney went immediately to St. Bonaventure's Monastery. He was so tired that he refused a meal; he wanted only to lie down. The Capuchin who greeted him showed him to his room, which had only an iron bed with a rough mattress, pillow and linens; a table; an armless chair and a curtainless window. Wondering what he had made his way into, he lay down and fell asleep.

Just before midnight the sound of chimes awakened him, and he found a procession of friars bearing candles to the chapel for midnight Mass. Barney joined them. The joyful celebration of the Christmas liturgy did much to lift his initial gloom.

The novice master deemed him a worthy candidate, and the Capuchin superiors decided to give Barney the Franciscan habit, which marked his entrance into the novitiate. But in the days between Christmas and the date of his official entrance into the novitiate, January 14, 1897, Barney's unease about what he was doing resurfaced. He called the eve of his receiving the Capuchin habit a "day of anxiety" and "dark indeed."[8]

However, "the moment I entered the Friars' Chapel to receive the habit," Solanus later wrote, "the struggle ceased and never troubled me again."[9] Barney took the name Francis Solanus, after the seventeenth-century Spaniard Francesco Solano, a Franciscan of great preaching ability who worked in Peru and, like Barney, played the violin, using it to teach catechism to children.

From his first days Solanus took to the Franciscan spirit, and it imbued his life. He would later express his sense of gratitude, a hallmark of his spirituality, and his personal connection to the Franciscan family: "How can we ever be [as] grateful as we ought to be for such a vocation to the Seraphic Order of the Poverello of Assisi?"[10]

In the words of Brother Leo Wollenweber, one of Solanus's secretaries and biographers and later the vice-postulator of his sainthood cause, "One of the most significant lessons of the novitiate was to learn the real meaning of the term 'Friars Minor,' which St. Francis gave to his followers. It means that Franciscans must consider themselves the least, not only of religious but also of all people. At the same time it means that they must be brothers to one another and to all creation. Solanus would grow in this spirit more and more throughout his life."[11] The minister general of the Capuchins one day would call him "an extraordinary man, a replica of St. Francis, a real Capuchin."[12]

The Question of Priesthood

Solanus was a conscientious and self-reflective novice who took his spiritual development seriously, and the rest of the community considered him a good candidate for making his first set of vows, which he did on July 14, 1897. At this point, however, a question arose, much as it did for Brother André when he was in the midst of his vow-taking. Did Solanus really have what it took to be a priest, especially intellectually?

His superiors also wondered what was most important to him: Had he entered the order to become a priest, or was it the Capuchin way of life that mattered most to him? To settle this matter Solanus signed a statement on the day before his first vows:

> I,...Solanus Casey, declare that I joined the Order of the Capuchins in the Province of St. Joseph with the pure intention to follow thus my religious vocation. Although I would wish and should be thankful, being admitted to the ordination of a priest, *considering the lack of my talents*, I leave it to my superiors to judge on my faculties and to dispose of me as they think best.
>
> I therefore will lay no claim whatsoever if they should think me not worthy or not able for the priesthood and I always will humbly submit to their appointments.[13]

Solanus's superiors wanted to have a basis on which to decide about his future. Were he to insist on pursuing ordination even if his study abilities were inadequate, they could dismiss him. But if he wanted to remain in the order whatever his status, he could stay.

In these words of Solanus we hear themes that remained with him for the next sixty years:

- **"Considering the lack of my talents."** According to Capuchin Father Michael Crosby, who has done extensive research and writing on Solanus and has worked on his sainthood cause, Solanus believed the evaluations of his superiors, which stated that he lacked full qualifications. As noted previously, he was a rather intelligent person, so the issue is less whether Solanus was really mentally lacking and more how he saw himself.

- **"I will always humbly submit to their appointments."** Throughout his life Solanus subscribed to the notion, common to Catholic religious of the era, of the absolute obedience owed to the superiors of one's community. Though he undoubtedly saw such obedience to be a virtue, there was more to it than simply following orders without question.

For Solanus one of the key values of life was *trust*. He trusted that whatever happened could be accepted. "Trust in God," he wrote. "His providence governs all things sweetly, even though we cannot see it immediately. This is where we must have faith and confidence."[14]

To Solanus's way of thinking, Michael Crosby writes, "the only things that could place obstacles to the power of God at work in the world were doubt and fear."[15] "One of humanity's greatest weaknesses is setting a limit on God's power and goodness," Solanus also said.[16] Trust, faith and humility were cut from the same cloth. To offer up one's own will, desires and even disappointments and losses was an act of faith, of trust in God's will, and an offering of oneself for the good of others.

Father Solanus

After he became a novice, Solanus traveled with his classmates from Detroit to Milwaukee to attend the Capuchin seminary at St. Francis Monastery, and there he entered into his studies for the priesthood. The train trip took place in hot July weather—in contrast, Solanus noted, to the blizzard he had ridden through going the other direction a year and a half earlier.

From early on things did not go well for Solanus at St. Francis. His grades in theology were subpar, and the questions about his capacity to complete the course of studies for the priesthood remained. The next set of vows, this time his solemn vows, precipitated another signed statement about what he would accept.

"I hereby declare," the statement of July 5, 1901, said, "(1) that I do not want to become a priest if my legitimate superiors consider me unqualified; (2) that I still wish to be able to receive one or the other of the orders [the minor orders leading to priesthood], but will be satisfied if they exclude me entirely from the higher orders. I have offered myself to God without reservation," he continued. "For that reason I leave it without anxiety to the superiors to decide about me as they may judge best before God."[17]

He took his solemn vows a little over two weeks later, and the following school year the community would allow him to receive orders. Writing of his probable ordination to the diaconate and the priesthood, he echoed the words of his statement in a letter to his sister: "May the Holy Ghost direct my superiors in their decision in this regard and may His Holy Will in all thingsbe done." Under his signature he wrote the word *resignation* and drew a cross.[18]

Without much change in his grades, Solanus moved toward ordination on uncertain ground. With remarkable insight, though, the director of studies, Father Anthony Rottensteiner, said, "We shall ordain...Solanus and as a priest he will be to the people something like the Curé of Ars."[19]

Rottensteiner was referring to Saint John Vianney, the nineteenth-century parish priest who served for forty years in the French town of Ars. Vianney was a farmhand and catechist who struggled as a student, particularly with Latin. At first he was not authorized to hear confessions or preach formal sermons, though he later gained permission to do these things and became famous for them. As a preacher and especially as a confessor, he had the spiritual gifts of prophecy and knowledge of hidden things, which Solanus was also to have.

As Solanus's ordination approached, he found himself in a group of three lagging students: himself, John O'Donovan and Damasus Wickland. The Capuchin superiors decided to ordain these three as what was then known as "simplex" priests. They could celebrate Mass, but they would not have permission to hear confessions or give formal sermons. O'Donovan contested this decision and later persuaded the order to allow him to preach, but Damasus and Solanus did not.

Solanus was a simplex priest the rest of his life. Father Rottensteiner's otherwise prescient prediction about him lacked a crucial point of comparison with the Curé: He would never hear confessions or preach.

On Sunday, July 24, 1904, in Milwaukee, the new archbishop, Sebastian Messmer, who was the brother of Solanus's former novice master, ordained him and his classmates. Following the Capuchin custom of the time, Solanus celebrated his first Mass a week later at the Capuchin church nearest his home, St. Joseph's in Appleton, Wisconsin.

These were days of great joy for him. His family came two hundred miles from Superior. Solanus had not seen his mother for eight years. His father wept throughout the entire liturgy "at the thought that God had finally blessed his family with a priest."[20] Maurice Casey had left the seminary, but that day he told Solanus that he had decided to try the priesthood again.

Almost immediately, Solanus received his first assignment: Sacred Heart parish in Yonkers, New York. He was to be there in four days.

CHAPTER THREE

Into the Mountains

Normally no one should have heard of him.

—John McCaffery, *Tales of Padre Pio*

While Padre Pio spent much of his life in the small mountain town of San Giovanni Rotondo, his life began in another small town, Pietrelcina, on May 25, 1887. He was the middle child of seven children, one of whom died in infancy, born to Grazio Forgione and Maria Giuseppa Di Nunzo, both in their twenties at the time. He was baptized on May 26, and his parents gave him the name Francesco, after Saint Francis of Assisi, a favorite saint of his mother.

Like André and Solanus, Pio was born into very simple, even primitive, surroundings. The family home consisted of a thirty-foot-square room with a dirt floor and one small window.

Both parents were very devout. People described Grazio as "simple," "lovely" and "holy." He stopped at church every day on his way home from working in the fields. He never swore, and he prayed the rosary often.[1]

In the manner of the other doorkeepers, Francesco was a pious and well-behaved child. "I never goofed off in my life," Pio said as an adult. He called himself "an unsalted piece of macaroni."[2] Like Brother André, he spent a lot of time praying in church, and though he had friends, his piety set him apart. For example, he did not go out and play with some of his friends because they swore.

It is clear that from an early age something spiritually unusual was going on with the boy Francesco. He began seeing apparitions and having other mystical experiences when he was only a few years old. Sometimes he beheld evil spirits tormenting him. He subjected himself to penances, such as sleeping on the floor instead of in his bed.

A dramatic childhood event had a deep effect on Francesco, much like Solanus's witnessing of an assault in front of the streetcar. On a pilgrimage with his father to the shrine of San Pellegrino, Francesco saw a desperate mother seeking the healing of her deformed child. He joined his prayers to those of the mother. Eventually the woman put the child on the altar and cried out to the saint, "Why don't you want to heal him for me?" At that the child "stood up, completely healed."[3]

The commotion the mother's pleas had caused was exceeded only by the response of the people to the healing. The combination of the mother's prayers and the dramatic restoration of the boy's body to wholeness impressed on Francesco the power of prayer and the possibility of God's healing in response to faith.

Brother Pio

As with the other doorkeepers, the need to work and help support his family interrupted Francesco's elementary education, but he pieced together a basic education with various teachers. By all accounts he was bright and a good student. For poor children of that time and place, the main way to pursue an education was to enter religious life or the priesthood.

His meeting with a young Capuchin Franciscan friar from the monastery of Morcone, Brother Camillo, suggested to him the idea of joining the Capuchins. When the provincial superior informed Francesco that there was no room for him in Morcone, his uncle advised him to look at another order. But Francesco was determined to "wear a beard like Brother Camillo."[4] Saint Francis of Assisi's influence on the imagination of Francesco's family may have also prompted his attraction to the Capuchins.

Finally a spot opened up in the Morcone friary, and the Capuchins gave Francesco a date in early January 1903 to join their novitiate. When the day came to leave Pietrelcina, his mother said to him, "Son, I can feel my heart breaking within me, but Saint Francis is calling and you must go."[5]

Thus Francesco entered the harsh novitiate of the turn-of-the-century Italian Capuchins. Theirs was an exacting schedule of prayer, study, strict discipline and occasional arbitrary and humiliating punishment. As for living conditions:

> Each novice had a tiny cell containing a bed, a chair, a table and a washstand holding a jug of cold water. The bedding

> was no more than a sack filled with corn husks lying on top
> of a board. Fra Pio slept on this in his clothes after prayers
> and a meticulous examination of conscience....The master
> of novices...wakened his charges at midnight to go sing
> lauds and matins in the choir. Shivering along the corri-
> dors in their bare feet, their teeth chattering with cold, and
> yawning with drowsiness, the friarlings staggered on to
> praise the Lord and thank Him for all His mercies.[6]

Despite the hardness of the life, Francesco took to the opportunity with great devotion and applied himself to his studies. As for the rules, restrictions and punishments, he told his novice friends, "The more ridiculous the order, the more willingly I obey it."[7] This embrace of obedience contrasted with the attitude of another young man, who left the novitiate after telling the novice master, "Back home in Naples we pay a dime to see madmen. Here we see them for free."[8]

At the beginning of the novitiate, Francesco received his Capuchin habit as well as the new name Pio. His superiors may have chosen this name for him because the relics of the early martyr Saint Pius resided at the Pietrelcina parish church.

A year later Pio and the other novices took their first vows and left for their next place of study, the Sant'Elia Monastery in Pianisi. There Pio spent six years studying philosophy, theology and the Franciscan rule. He spent a year of this time studying in the San Marco la Catola Friary ten miles away.

Pio was a diligent, "ordinary" student who distinguished himself by his conduct. "Amidst the lively, noisy students, he was quiet and calm....He was always humble, meek, and obedient."[9] Interestingly, Pio never took the necessary courses to preach; like Solanus Casey, he never received church license to give formal sermons as a Capuchin.

Spiritual Stirrings

In 1907, after a year back at Sant'Elia, Pio professed his permanent vows. He had been an exemplary novice. The next few years, spanning his preparation for the priesthood, his ordination and his early years as a priest, would see the young friar's life become more and more complicated and unusual.

The first issue was Pio's health. Like Brother André, he began to experience severe digestive problems, and for periods of time he was unable to keep down much food. He suffered from intense headaches and tired easily. Some people thought he had contracted tuberculosis; this suspicion led to an initial ban on his hearing confessions. His condition became so severe at times that some thought he would die.

These illnesses caused his superiors to move him to monasteries in healthier climates and even allow him to live and study at home in Pietrelcina. It was extraordinary treatment for a junior friar. Strangely, his illnesses sometimes ebbed and flowed with where he was: "Hardly did he arrive in [the] friary than he began to vomit. Yet as soon as he sets foot on his native soil, his stomach recovers," wrote the superior of the monastery at Venafro, where Pio lived off and on for a while.[10]

His stays at home in Pietrelcina continued even after his ordination in 1910. There he would celebrate Mass almost daily—some days going out to rural parishes.

He also taught school, organized a boys' choir and held classes in the fields to teach adults to read and write.

Amazing things started happening. In his prayer Pio sometimes fell into ecstasies in which he had visions of Christ and the Blessed Virgin Mary. He described his prayer like this: "Hardly do I begin to pray than at once I feel my soul begin to recollect itself in a peace and tranquillity that I cannot express in words. The senses remain suspended, with the exception of my hearing, which sometimes is not suspended; yet…even if a great deal of noise were made around me, this would not bother me in the slightest."

He experienced a "continuous thought of God," a sense of being "totally lost in God." "All this arises," he said, "not from my own mental efforts or preparation, but from an internal flame and from a love so powerful that if God did not quickly come to my aid, I would be consumed!"[11]

Pio also engaged in battle with what appeared to be evil spirits that assaulted him, usually at night. These struggles were quite physical, and the noise from them was loud enough to be heard by many others, frequently to their great alarm.

Other spiritual patterns formed. The Masses he celebrated were long. People began to associate miracles of healing and deliverance with him, and he manifested gifts of prophecy and the ability to read others' thoughts.

In September of 1910, only a month after his ordination in the cathedral at Benevento, he received an early version of the stigmata during a vision of Jesus and Mary. At the time of his ordination, Pio had "offered himself formally as a victim for the salvation of sinners."[12] Now it appeared that God had responded to this self-offering by allowing Pio to follow in the footsteps of his spiritual father Saint Francis of Assisi and share in the passion of Jesus in a special way.

Pio's reaction to this experience showed his humility as well as the burden he felt this gift to be. He went to Father Salvatore Pannullo, the priest in Pietrelcina the parishioners called "Uncle Sal," who had become a second father to Francesco when Grazio had worked in the United States. Together Pio and *Pati* ("little father"), as Pio called him,[13] prayed. Pio asked his fellow priest, "Father, do me a favor. Ask Jesus to take them away. I want to suffer, to die from suffering, but in secret."[14]

The physical stigmata disappeared, but their pain remained.

Father Pannullo also had to handle an early accusation against Pio. A former schoolmate sent an anonymous letter to Pannullo saying that Pio was having a sexual relationship with the stationmaster's daughter. The priest took the accusations seriously, but eventually the man confessed to making up the story, and Pio was cleared.

A New Home

Pio's spiritual reputation attracted attention. From the monastery at Foggia, he wrote his spiritual director, "If you don't hear very often from me, don't blame me. I don't have a moment of free time. Crowds of people thirsting for Jesus are flocking to me so that I would lay hands on them."[15]

One hot summer day in 1916, the Capuchin Padre Paolino came through Foggia and visited Padre Pio. He suggested they both move on for a visit to the mountain town of San Giovanni Rotondo. With his superior's permission, Padre Pio accompanied Padre Paolino to San Giovanni and the Capuchin monastery there, Our Lady of Grace.

San Giovanni is located in the Gargano Mountains on the "spur" of the Italian peninsula, which sticks out sixty-five miles into the Adriatic Sea. It is arid and bleak land. In the winter it snows, and cold winds blow off the sea, while the summers are scorching hot. As for the wildlife, "cicadas cluster in their millions in the thorny scrub. Huge lizards abound, and horned vipers take their ease, curled up on hot stones in the sun. Birds of every kind raise their young in the spiny gorse and thorn bushes, and high above all of this intense, throbbing life cruise the hawks."[16]

The five-hundred-year-old Monastery of Our Lady of Grace is about a mile from San Giovanni Rotondo, accessible at that time only by a mule track. Given its poverty and location, most considered an assignment there a punishment. But after a week's visit, Padre Pio liked it. On his return to Foggia he requested a permanent transfer there. "Jesus is calling me to do so," he said.[17]

The increasing numbers of people who were coming to see Pio at the monastery in Foggia had started to disrupt the life there. His superiors, divided on whether his developing gifts really came from God, decided that a reassignment to Our Lady of Grace would be wise. Besides taking Pio out of Foggia, the move could serve as a kind of discerning of spirits: If Pio's gifts were the real thing, they would flourish even in this harsh ground; if they weren't, they would wither.

As Pio's spiritual daughter Katharina Tangari put it, "The choice of an obscure little monastery in the harsh, inhospitable Gargano region seemed to resolve the Padre Pio question for good."[18]

The Doorkeepers

Padre Pio, Brother André and Father Solanus knew hard work, meager circumstances, losses and illness. They had to struggle to get to the places they knew they wanted to be. But from the beginning they also had great faith and prayerfulness. Devout and obedient, they felt most at home in the church. They loved to talk of God.

Throughout their lives they showed this same faith, devotion to God and others and patience in the face of suffering. They embraced their lowliness rather than trying to overcome it. Their faith expressed itself in true humility: a total giving of themselves to God and other people.

"The kingdom of God…is like a mustard seed, which, when sown upon the ground, is the smallest of all the seeds on earth; yet when it is sown it grows up and becomes the greatest of all shrubs" (Mark 4:30–32). Out of the tiny seeds of their lives grew great trees of prayer, healing and faith that sheltered millions seeking the mercy and presence of God.

PART TWO

EVERYDAY MIRACLES

CHAPTER FOUR

"Get Up and Walk"

*I would not finish if I tried to tell you all the
marvels and graces done here by our
good and powerful St. Joseph.*

—Brother Aldéric, confrere of Brother André Bessette

Once Brother André had joined the Holy Cross community as a vowed member, he settled into his round of work and prayer. Perhaps the only thing extraordinary about this lowly figure was his great piety and his unswerving humility, obedience and willingness to do whatever others expected of him.

It is fitting that some of the first evidence of the unusual grew out of his everyday tasks. In 1871, a year after André joined the community, a smallpox outbreak occurred, and several students and teachers at the Holy Cross school at St-Laurent came down with the disease. To help care for the sick, Brother André's superiors temporarily sent him to St-Laurent.

While there, Brother André suggested that the healthy members of the community carry a statue of Saint

Joseph around the building in prayer. This practice was not new. Only a year before the same community had walked in procession during another epidemic. But this time all those who had contracted smallpox grew better, and no one else became ill from the disease.

In League With Saint Joseph

Of course it is more difficult to attribute this positive outcome to Brother André's role than it is to see his hand in favors later in his ministry, when the afflicted came to him. But it is intriguing to ponder the possibility that Brother André, already deeply devoted to Saint Joseph, was beginning to have a sense of special connection with the healing power of God through the saint. Was André's unique relationship with Joseph manifesting itself, even in such a way that few noted André's part in it?

In 1870 Pope Pius IX had proclaimed Saint Joseph, guardian of the Holy Family and earthly father of Jesus, to be the patron of the universal church. Devotion to Joseph was not new to French Canada or the Holy Cross order. The first missionaries to arrive in Canada, the Récollets, consecrated the French colony to Joseph. One of the founders of Montréal established the Religious Hospitallers of Saint Joseph, and one of the city's first churches and first streets bore the name Saint Joseph. What is more, Holy Cross as a community and the order's founder, Father Basile Moreau, had a devotion to Saint Joseph.

The use of Saint Joseph's oil for curative purposes was common in France, Canada and even the college in which André lived and worked, where several oil-related healings had occurred.[1] The Brothers of Holy Cross had brought with them from France the practices of blessing the sick with oil that had burned before an image of Saint Joseph and touching the skin of the sick with a Saint Joseph medal.

As for his personal devotion to the saint, Brother André's friend Joseph Pichette made this telling remark: "Saint Joseph had lived a hidden life and [Brother André] viewed this as an example to follow."[2]

André considered Saint Joseph a personal friend, and he spoke to him as to a friend. In this relationship, forged in André's early years and confirmed in his vocation, lay his utter confidence in turning to Saint Joseph as his personal patron, in recommending the saint's healing power to others and in his later determination to build a lasting place of prayer to him.

André recommended Saint Joseph's oil to the students, and sometimes he anointed them or touched them with a medal himself. "If he was cutting a boy's hair, for example, and the boy complained of a toothache, Brother André touched the boy's face with a medal."[3] André advised those facing family problems, lawsuits or difficult business encounters to hold a Saint Joseph medal in their hands as they dealt with these situations.

"Go and Play!"

Many of the healings that came through Brother André's intercession involved telling people that they were not sick or disabled, even though they seemed to be in the grip of illness or a crippling physical problem. He would say to the afflicted, "You don't feel any pain," or,

"You're not sick."

One of André's biographers, Father Jean-Guy Dubuc, tells of the healing of a student at the college:

> While at the infirmary watching over a few patients, he came to the bed of a boy who, under doctor's orders, had been lying there for the last several days because of a strong fever, and said to him, "Why are you being so lazy?" To which the child replied, "But I'm sick." "No, you're not.... Why don't you go and play with the others?" And the boy, feeling a sudden strength, got up and joined his friends, to the astonishment of students and professors alike. The Brother's gesture was not appreciated. He was accused of being imprudent, and of interfering with the work of the head nurse. The boy was thoroughly examined, but not a trace of his former illness could be found. A doctor even checked on him several times a day, expecting some sort of relapse. But there was none. The sick boy was cured, and no one really knew how.[4]

One day in 1884 André was scrubbing floors when a woman suffering from disabling rheumatism was brought to him on a stretcher. To the men carrying her he said, "Let her walk by herself." After she took a few tentative steps, André went back to his work, and a little while later he said, "You're no longer sick. You can go home now."[5]

On another occasion, in 1918, Brother André was leaving his office for lunch when he passed a paralyzed American man tied to a stretcher and waiting to see him. As André started up the stairs of the rectory, he said in a casual way, "Untie him." When those with the afflicted man did so, he rose and walked. The resulting uproar from the people gathered was apparently lost on Brother André, who had already gone in to eat.

When André told the sick, in an almost offhand manner, to continue on as if they were no longer afflicted, one might say that he was helping them to recover the original health and wholeness they had or should have had.

Brother Aldéric, who had come to Canada with the first group of Holy Cross brothers and priests in 1847, reported healings of people in the village of Côtes-des-Neiges: cures of an eye infection, crippling arthritis and diphtheria. "I stop," Aldéric wrote. "I would not finish if I tried to tell you all the marvels and graces done here by our good and powerful St. Joseph."[6] At first people did not always mention André's name in connection with cures at Notre-Dame-des-Neiges, but as time went on, people began to recognize the part his prayers played.

Skeptics, Scoffers and Fearmongers

As in the healing of the feverish student, André's ministry occasionally encountered opposition. On the one hand some people simply were hostile to the possibility of cures related to faith. The persuasive power of a cure could overcome this skepticism.

One man whose two boys were enrolled at the college bristled whenever Brother André asked how things were going at home. Finally the man admitted that he was under great stress trying to pay for his sons' education as well as the medical care of his chronically ill wife. André told him, "At this very hour, things are better with you at home. Tell me about it the next time you come to see your boys."[7] When the man arrived home, his formerly bedridden wife greeted him on the front porch.

A thornier source of hostility had to do with Brother André's use of blessed oil. Both medals and oil are *sacramentals*—objects that, accompanied by prayers and rites, confer the blessing of God and lead to a sacramental awareness of his presence. Blessed oil, of course, is part of the celebration of several sacraments, including the anointing of the sick. As we have already noted, the Holy Cross community had made ample use of it for years. Nonetheless, André's practice made some members of the community uncomfortable. They began to call him the "Old Smearer" or the "Old Greaser."[8]

Such criticisms hurt André deeply. "Brother André used to weep," a member of his community reported, "simply because he was so hurt. But he never criticized anyone, and he never held a grudge."[9] Told of some derogatory names people called him, André tearfully said, "I don't know what I did to them. I don't know why they give me such a hard time. Is it then such a great harm to pray to St. Joseph with the sick?"[10]

Regarding the Saint Joseph medal and oil, André said, "The medal is only metal. The oil is just olive oil. But it makes [people] think more about Saint Joseph and so strengthens their faith."[11]

Other opposition came from outside the Holy Cross community. By 1890, with larger and larger numbers of the sick congregating on the college grounds, some parents were expressing concern that the boys might contract diseases from visitors. They worried about the sick people who found their way into the building and wandered the hallways in search of Brother André.

A group of physicians declared Brother André ignorant and a danger to the public health. He responded, "They are right. I am ignorant. That is the reason why the Good God concerns himself with me. If there was anyone more ignorant than I, the Good God would choose him instead of me."[12]

The development of the local transportation system and the clever thinking of the college superior intervened in Brother André's difficulties. In 1897 a new tramway line connected the campus with downtown Montréal, and the railroad built a small station right in front of the entrance to the college. The college superior had the idea of letting Brother André use the station to receive visitors. So for the next twelve years people met Brother André in what one writer called his "first reception room," now a safe distance from students and scoffers alike.[13]

The Daily Routine

On most days Brother André rose by 5:00 AM, cleaned his room and then went to the chapel for two hours of prayer. In his office at nine, he received the afflicted until noon, then again from two to five. Some days Brother André received people only until 3:00 PM, then led an hour of prayer, during which guests prayed for particular people and expressed their gratitude to God.

Those wishing to see Brother André climbed a low flight of stairs to the waiting room of his office. In the days before handicap accessibility, people ascended any way they could—even if others had to carry them.

A window connected the office and the waiting room. When André received women, he opened the window so as to be visible to the people waiting. The office itself was fairly small. On one wall hung a crucifix; on the other walls were images of Saint Joseph and Christ before Pilate.

André stood behind a counter to see visitors. He began every session by telling the person to desire the holy will of God. He might say, "God expects you to do something for Him. He died because He has need of souls, and this is what He expects of you."[14]

André told people to pray and make novenas to Saint Joseph. Sometimes he recommended this simple prayer: "Saint Joseph, pray for me as you yourself would have prayed if you had been in my place, in the same situation. Saint Joseph, hear me!"[15]

The conversations Brother André had with visitors "were as brief as they were kind, and the sick left invigorated, feeling lighter in both body and soul."[16] André's ringing of a little bell signaled the end of a visit and told the next person in line to come forward.

Following his evening meal (unless it was Friday, when he participated in the stations of the cross), one of his lay friends drove him to area hospitals, nursing homes and private homes on a list his superior gave him each day. André's availability earned him a new and better nickname: "Our Family Physician."

Returning home between nine and ten o'clock, he and whoever drove him that day prayed for about an hour for those whom André had visited. In the words of biographer Sister Claire Vanier, Brother André "loved to talk to God about the suffering people he had encountered during the day but he also listened to God in order to receive the messages of hope that he wished to pass on to those who would come to him the following day."[17] Father Solanus Casey also followed the practice of praying in the chapel in the evening for all the needs people had brought him that day.

Knowing God's Will

The number of reported healings from 1910 to the end of Brother André's life is quite large. Some estimates run to ten thousand, or about four hundred per year—more than one a day. Infections disappeared, polio and meningitis left the bodies of children, those unable to walk cast aside their crutches, maimed limbs became whole and normal.

In an especially charming story, a woman brought her four-year-old niece, who could not walk, to Brother André. "Put her down," he said. "You don't carry a child who has all her limbs."

On her first attempt to walk, the child collapsed. The aunt stood the child up again, and André, holding a medal of Saint Joseph, told her, "Come and get the medal." She walked over to Brother André. He gave her the medal and said, "Bring it back when you're seven." Her cure was not at first total, but her experience with Brother André set her on the road to the complete ability to walk.[18]

Some cures were not instantaneous or complete. His friend Joseph Pichette, a storekeeper, said thirty years after André prayed with him, "Though I was not entirely cured, I could still work without too much pain."[19] In another case a blind person regained his sight but not completely. Others experienced healing over a period of time.

Archbishop Bruchési of Montréal once asked Brother André, "In some cases you tell the sick, 'You're cured,' and it is done. To others you advise to pray to Saint Joseph, to make novenas, to others you say to rub with a medal, to use the oil of St. Joseph, to others you say, 'I'm going to pray for you.' What is the reason for the difference?"

To the archbishop André said, "There are times when it is easy to see." He would also say, "In some cases it is evident that St. Joseph wants to heal them," or, "It is according to the will of God. When it is good for their salvation, the Good God lets me see that it is not his will. I do not want to go against him," or, "When I tell them, 'Let go of your crutches,' it is because it is evident." In short, "I say what I am told to say."[20]

A very important aspect of André's ministry emerges from these answers. He had a profound spiritual intuition about people's situations. Although André never claimed to receive visions or hear the divine voice, he clearly had a supernatural ability to read the situations of those who visited him. Somehow God or Saint Joseph was telling him what was to be.

CHAPTER FIVE

"Thank God Ahead of Time"

*God knows best, and, while we'll still hope for a
favorable surprise, we can hardly do better
than not only being resigned to whatever
God permits but even beforehand to
thank Him for His mercifully
loving designs.*

—Solanus Casey, letter to a person in Detroit

Solanus's struggle to find his place as a priest and member of the Capuchins followed him, in a sense, to his first assignment. Sacred Heart parish in the New York suburb of Yonkers, where Solanus arrived in 1904, looked down from a hill onto the Hudson River. The view from his window reminded Solanus of his childhood home in Wisconsin.

Solanus's simplex status presented a problem to the pastor of Sacred Heart, Father Bonaventure Frey. Father Frey, who had cofounded the Capuchin order in the United States and established the parish, had admitted Solanus into the Capuchin novitiate seven years earlier in Detroit. Now he was faced with the question of how to employ an apparently holy priest who could not do the regular parish work of hearing confessions and preaching at Masses.

Father Bonaventure ended up putting Solanus in charge of the church's sacristy and of the altar boys. In this and in his future assignments, Solanus, though a member of the clergy who had studied theology for ten years, performed the tasks of unordained brothers.

Solanus was strict but fair with the boys, quick to reproach them for lack of reverence in their tasks but also eager to reward them for good service with walks to the park, stops for ice cream and subway trips to the beach, Manhattan, St. Patrick's Cathedral and baseball games. The boys knew he cared about them, and they loved playing baseball with the catcher who refused to wear a mask.

The Holy Priest

After a couple of years Father Frey retired, and a new pastor, Father Aloysius Blonigen, came to Sacred Heart. Quite soon he gave Solanus a new assignment: that of porter for the monastic community and the church office.

As porter Solanus answered the door, tracked down friars who had visitors and handled messages and packages. He swept the sidewalk in the morning and talked with people in the neighborhood. Sometimes he ran inside and came out with food to give away. Other times people asked him to visit an afflicted person at home. He became known as "the holy priest," as in "Go get the holy priest," when someone was in need.

Especially when people were sick, more and more often someone came to the monastery and asked for Solanus. People noted his sensitivity and gentleness. "If you were sick, he hurt with you. He was very compassionate. He could say a few words to you and you would be perfectly at ease."[1]

Solanus demonstrated an openness to all people, including non-Catholics. At this early point in his ministry, his visiting took him to non-Catholic homes where Catholic servants who belonged to the parish were employed. In time Protestants, Jews, people of many faiths and races as well as nonbelievers came to see him. While inviting non-Catholics to consider the "claims" of the Catholic faith, he respected people's religious commitments and encouraged them to live up to those commitments. Commenting on his definition of religion, "the science of our happy relationship with God and our neighbors," Solanus wrote, "There *can be but one religion*, though there may be a thousand different systems of religion."[2]

One woman saw a rabbi with a cane come to visit Solanus every week. "Now he had faith and I was full of doubts," the woman said. "But when I saw him walk away *without* the use of his cane, then I believed."[3]

The other doorkeepers embodied this same ecumenical spirit. André invited everyone to pray at the oratory, including Protestants and Jews. Many Protestant military personnel attended Pio's Masses during World War II; he was reportedly friendly with all of them (though he had little patience for Jehovah's Witnesses) and never pressured them to convert to Catholicism. "If they intend to convert," he said, "the Lord will show a way."[4]

In the context of everyday acts of concern and service, Solanus's gifts began to make themselves known. He once went to visit a woman who had given birth and was suffering from a life-threatening infection. He immediately asked for holy water. The family had none, so he sent Carmella Petrosino, a girl who acted as a go-between and translator for Solanus and the Italian immigrants in the parish, to her home to get some. When she returned, Solanus prayed over the sick woman and blessed her, "and from then on the woman got over her infection and lived a long time afterward."[5]

During the World War I years, he developed the habit of visiting families in the parish who had men going into the armed forces. Solanus would pray with the family for their safety and bless the departing men. Sometimes he would predict their safe return.

The Sisters of St. Agnes, who served the parish, noticed this ability to predict the future. They would say to one another, "If in June, when you go back to the motherhouse in Wisconsin, Father Solanus says, 'See you in September,' you will be coming back; if he just says 'Goodbye,' you will be transferred."[6]

Solanus just seemed to know. As his ministry developed, he gave prophetic words of encouragement to many: "Tomorrow at 9 o'clock," "in two days at 3 o'clock," or "within a short time," "if you have faith these troubles will disappear."[7]

Perhaps this prescient gift served Solanus's own well-being when his parents celebrated their fiftieth wedding anniversary. He made the long trip to Seattle for the event, where he celebrated Mass with his two priest brothers, Maurice and Edward. A program of tributes, songs and poetry followed.

It was the last time Solanus would see his parents. Two years later his father died while saying a prayer to Our Lady of Sorrows. Three years after that his mother died of pneumonia during the noontime ringing of the Angelus bells. Though Solanus could not be present for their funerals, the memory of their anniversary celebration was perhaps a great comfort. And the circumstances surrounding their deaths served as reminders of the gift of faith they had given him.

The Front-Door Ministry

In July 1918, after Solanus had served for fourteen years at Sacred Heart, his superiors transferred him to a Capuchin parish in lower Manhattan, Our Lady of Sorrows. His new assignment began the same day as the transfer. His journey from the country to the suburbs to the city was now complete.

Father Venantius Buessing, his new superior, made him the sacristan, as he had once been in Yonkers, and also director of a parish young woman's group, or sodality. Though Solanus could not preach formal homilies, he could deliver short exhortations, known as "ferverinos," to this group on the Scripture for the day. Solanus worked hard on these "homilettes," frequently speaking of God's love and the challenge to accept and respond to it. About fourteen of the homilies have been preserved.

At Our Lady of Sorrows Solanus had more time to himself, and these three years in the heart of the city were a kind of retreat for him. He studied Scripture and read piles of books dealing with the saints, the church fathers and mystical writings. He also devoted himself to personal prayer.

The provincial chapter of 1921 moved Solanus yet again, sending him to the Capuchin parish of Our Lady, Queen of Angels in Harlem, where he resumed the duties of porter. Starting in Yonkers, but especially in Harlem and later when he returned to Detroit, his front-door ministry took on the form that it would have for the rest of his life.

Solanus sat in an office near the door. People came and waited to talk with him. In their time with him they told him of their problems: sick loved ones, marital troubles, estranged family members, unemployment, looming surgeries, drinking problems, depression, anxiety. Invariably Solanus listened with attention. He sometimes laid his hands on a sick person and prayed. In other cases he promised to pray for the person's needs, which he did in the chapel after he had fulfilled his other responsibilities.

After hearing about a difficult situation, sometimes Solanus looked away into space. It seemed he would receive an intuition. He could see into the problem, what the need was and how it would turn out. Returning to the person, he would speak very gently and with great compassion, offering advice and comfort.

Solanus encouraged his visitors to "do something to please the Dear Lord"[8] as a sign of faith and commitment, like helping the needy, going to confession, returning to regular prayer and participation in the sacraments. He often persuaded them to join the Seraphic Mass Association (SMA). Founded in Switzerland at the turn of the twentieth century, the association raised money to support Capuchin missions throughout the world. In exchange for a small contribution, Capuchins worldwide would remember SMA members in Masses and other prayers.

Solanus saw many values in the SMA. It supported the Capuchin missions, encouraged appreciation for the benefits of the Mass and the mission of the church and gave the people he talked with a way to give as well as ask for something. So many new SMA memberships came in through Solanus's work that he became an official promoter of the association. People tended to want Solanus rather than another friar to sign them up for the SMA, as more favors seemed to flow for the members he enrolled.

Solanus also visited inmates at a Harlem prison. Now he went to minister to, not guard, the prisoners, who were largely poor African Americans. He said Mass, talked with them, gave them newspapers and Christmas cards and administered "the pledge"—a promise not to drink for a certain time after they were released from jail.

Answers to Prayer

Solanus's ministry at the front door produced results. Sick relatives became better. Estranged spouses reconciled. Personal problems resolved themselves. People were coming back to Solanus to tell him about these favors and blessings. "Thank God!" and "God is good!" Solanus would say. He reminded them that the blessing came not from him but from God, and through the many Capuchin priests around the world who had offered Masses for their intentions.

Solanus had been noting answers to prayers as early as 1901. Perhaps he had some inkling of his gifts even as a novice, when he wrote in his notebook, "Beware of congratulating thyself on the blessings wrought through thy medium."[9]

When the Capuchin provincial, Father Benno Aichinger, visited the friary in Harlem in 1923, he told Solanus to begin keeping a record of his visits with people. Ever obedient and dutiful, Solanus acquired a notebook and wrote under the first entry: "Nov. 8th, 1923....Father Provincial wishes notes to be made of special favors reported through the Seraphic Mass Association." For example, a woman enrolled her sister, who suffered from severe pain, and later reported, "Thank God and the good prayer society, I'm feeling fine."[10] Every third or fourth entry recorded a similar positive outcome.[11]

By 1956 Solanus had filled seven of these "Notebooks of Favors Reported" with more than six thousand entries. At that time one of Solanus's assistants, Father Blase Gitzen, had so many reports of cures through the intercession of Solanus that he "eventually threw them away."[12]

The number of Solanus's visitors continued to grow, but in July 1924 he found out that he was to move from New York to the Capuchins' provincial headquarters in Detroit, St. Bonaventure's Monastery. In the peremptory ways of religious life in those days, he received the news on July 30 and had to be in Detroit on August 1. He packed immediately and was on the train the next day.

At St. Bonaventure's Solanus became an assistant to the longtime porter, Brother Francis Spruck, and picked up where he had left off in New York. It didn't take long for large numbers of people to begin coming to talk with him. Soon the friars left the door unlocked and put a sign over the doorbell that said, "Walk In."

Some days Solanus's time in the office lasted from 7:00 AM to 10:00 PM. "From morning to night he would be listening to persons with worries and cares and disturbances, and with all the humility and all the patience in the world he would give them fatherly advice and often enkindle their courage and hope and reassure them in a brief time their troubles would be finished or counsel them to be resigned to suffer with Christ."[13] Solanus's evening prayer for people stretched his day out to as much as eighteen hours.

Though thousands of people poured out their hearts to him, Solanus could not give absolution for sins because of his simplex status. Instead he worked out a system with one of the other priests, such as Father Herman Buss at St. Bonaventure's. After hearing a petitioner's story, he would say, "Now go over to the church and I'll call Father Herman and he'll go over to hear your confession....Now you told the whole story. Just give a résumé to Father Herman. He will understand that you talked to me and he'll give you absolution."[14]

Following God's Plan

Visits with Solanus in his office frequently concluded with his giving a blessing. In the words of Brother Leo Wollenweber, "Standing—a tall, thin, almost gaunt figure—he would place his hands with their crooked arthritic fingers on the head of the person and softly pray. Sometimes he might playfully tap the person on the head or cheek" and give the person a smile, accompanied by his "twinkling blue eyes."[15]

"When he was speaking with you," another Capuchin said, "you felt that he was constantly God-centered, on fire with love for God, and constantly God-conscious, seeming always to have his eyes on God. He seemed to see everything as flowing from God and leading back to God."[16]

Solanus never seemed to lose patience under the crush of visitors, despite the long hours he kept. And his patience spawned patience in the people waiting to see him. They knew that he had time for them, and he treated each as if he or she were the most important person in the world. Even when people had to wait for hours, they remained peaceful. "Somehow the sense was that Solanus would take as much time with every-body as was needed, and that somehow this was all part of God's plan."[17]

Rarely did Solanus speak of the hardships of his ministry. In a letter to his past assistant Brother Leo, he qualified his "complaint" by pointing out that his calling far outweighed the pain he experienced: "Even though fraught with dangers, it has many advantages, if only we be of good will, and cooperate with the graces never failing on God's part and [that of] our Blessed Mother. Sometimes of course it becomes monotonous and extremely boring, till one is nearly collapsing."[18] But with typical humility Solanus added, "In such cases it helps to remember that even when Jesus was about to fall the third time, he patiently consoled the women folk and children of his persecutors, making no exception."[19]

"That poor sinner Solanus," he once told Brother Leo, "more than anyone else gave me trouble as long as I was in St. Bonaventure's."[20] Deflecting the focus from those who burdened him with their troubles, he once asked someone to "Breathe a little [prayer] for the conversion of the poor sinner Solanus who makes so little progress in faith, hope, and charity."[21]

On the Move Again

In July of 1945 the Capuchins unexpectedly moved Solanus to St. Michael's Monastery in Brooklyn, New York. This transfer, coming after Solanus's twenty-one years in Detroit, was an attempt to ease the burdens on him and give him a chance to get more rest. "I guess they thought I was too besieged by the people in Detroit," he said.[22]

Another issue played a role in Solanus's transfer. For many years he had been a devotee of a massive work by the Spanish mystic Mary of Agreda called *The Mystical City of God*. Mary of Agreda claimed to be reporting the private revelations she had received regarding the life of the Blessed Virgin Mary. Solanus set great store by this work, had read it several times, more than once while on his knees, and recommended it to others.

The book was expensive and presented quite a challenge to the average reader, and many were skeptical of it and its author. Problems developed when people started complaining to the archdiocese of Detroit about the price of the book.

In addition, Ray Garland, who had helped Solanus in several ways, began promoting and selling the book. Garland also took part in a group devoted to *The*

Mystical City that attended Solanus's Masses at a local parish. This group continued to meet at the parish even after Solanus had to go away for some medical treatment, a move that angered the pastor and prompted a complaint to the Capuchins.

Transferring Solanus, though it was a shock to his many friends there, not only helped ease the demands on him but also spared him and the Capuchins any further difficulties over *The Mystical City*. His superior in Detroit said Solanus took word of this unexpected development as if someone had told him it was time for the next meal.[23] At once he began packing, and he was in Brooklyn two days later.

Writing back to St. Bonaventure's, Solanus admitted that he had been tired and that he welcomed the rest. But a rest it was not to be. Though he had been gone from the New York area for over twenty years, word spread quickly that Father Solanus was back in town, and before long the St. Michael's doorbell was ringing and mail was finding its way to him. In less than a year his superiors moved him again, this time to St. Felix Friary in Huntington, Indiana, the Capuchin novitiate house.

In Huntington Solanus worked in the friary garden and tended the beehives. The bees were docile around him, and once, when they threatened to swarm, Solanus calmed them by playing his harmonica. The pastoral activities and setting recalled for Solanus in a happy way his rural upbringing and gave him the opportunity to express his awe for God the Creator in the surroundings of the friary. He even revisited his baseball playing by joining in the novices' games, finding that he could still hit the occasional long drive.

But Huntington was only two hundred miles from Detroit, and Solanus could not retire there from his ministry. Soon calls started coming in for him, and people from Detroit made the trip, some in groups on chartered buses. There was no rest yet for Solanus. He would continue serving his Lord until the end of his days.

Chapter Six

A Holy and Living Sacrifice

*My past, O Lord, to thy mercy, my present to
thy love, my future to thy providence!*

—a prayer Padre Pio recommended to penitents

When the Duchess of St. Albans, an English follower of Padre Pio, visited San Giovanni Rotondo after his death to research her book about Pio, she talked with Father Joseph Pius, an American Capuchin who had come to live at the monastery in the padre's last years and who had become one of his close associates. Father Joseph and the duchess were talking about the miracles when she said that her approach would be to "write it as I go along and let the readers make up their own minds. They can take it or leave it. It's up to them. I am not out to convert anyone.

"This little speech of mine," she wrote, "[was] received without comment."[1]

Even Padre Pio and those close to him were wary of the impression he was creating. As one woman who had experienced a miracle said, "I've always been careful about telling my story. It's easy for people to think you're some kind of fanatic."[2]

Concerning how to talk about the miracles, a fellow Capuchin priest remarked, "You just have to go easy in the beginning....Today we are all suffering from spiritual starvation, and you shouldn't give a starving person too big a meal right away."[3]

Some have no problem accepting the fact that Saint Francis of Assisi and others who lived long ago bore the stigmata or that Saint Anthony of Padua had the gift of bilocation and could work wonders. Perhaps the resistance some people have today to saints like Padre Pio, André and Solanus comes from a discomfort with the idea that God is present, active and working miracles *today*.

These wonder-workers are not comfortably confined to the past; they exist within living memory. We can talk to people who knew them. We can look at photographs, even films, of them. The same kinds of wonders of old are happening in our time, for us, though we may find it hard to accept the fact that God is gracing us in these ways.

Sharing Christ's Wounds

In San Giovanni Padre Pio had the experience that literally marked him for the rest of his life. He had received the stigmata previously, though in answer to his prayers the physical signs had disappeared. But in August 1918, while hearing one of the seminarians' confessions, he had a vision of a "heavenly being" who stabbed him with a sword and inflicted on him an agony that lasted for two days.

About a month and a half later, on September 20, Pio was praying by himself in the monastery chapel. He described what happened in a letter to his spiritual director:

I was sitting in the choir, after celebrating Holy Mass,
when I was overtaken by a repose, similar to a deep sleep.
All of my senses…as well as the faculties of my soul were
steeped in an indescribable peace. As I was in this state, I
saw before my very eyes a mysterious Being…[who] had
blood dripping from his hands, feet, and side. His look
frightened me. I experienced something that I don't know
how to describe. I felt like I was dying, and I would have
died if the Lord had not intervened to strengthen my heart,
which was ready to burst out of my chest.

When the mysterious creature left, I found that my
hands, feet, and side had been pierced and were bleeding.
Imagine the anguish that I experienced at that moment and
that I have been experiencing continually since then.[4]

Padre Pio, who at his ordination had offered himself
as a sacrifice for the salvation of others, received, as if
in confirmation of his vocation, the wounds of Christ,
whose sacrifice had saved the world. His sensation of
nearly dying makes sense if he indeed was becoming a
living sacrifice for the good of others.

How did Pio react to what had happened? Much as
he had when the stigmata had first visited him. In his
letter he wrote, "[The Lord] can even leave the anguish
and the pain, but let him take away these visible signs
that are a source of embarrassment for me and an indescribable and unbearable humiliation."[5]

The date of the letter shows that Pio waited more
than a month to tell his superiors about what had happened. He tried to conceal his wounds by wrapping
them with bandages and handkerchiefs, but the other
monks noticed these efforts as well as spots of blood on

the floor and the difficulty with which Pio moved about the monastery.

Eventually Padre Paolino, the community's superior, demanded to know what was going on, and Pio showed him the wounds. Paolino informed the superior general, who came to the monastery to see the wounds himself. He ordered the community to keep secret the existence of Padre Pio's wounds and to proceed very carefully in regard to the situation. Yet word of Pio's gift inevitably began to spread outside the monastery, especially because the padre bled visibly while he celebrated Mass.

What did the stigmata look like? A professor wrote this description:

> Anatomically the stigmata are genuine lacerations of the soft tissue that are not produced by external agents or by disease, and that manifest themselves in an unforeseen way in predetermined places on the body. They appear suddenly and unexpectedly, and are preceded and accompanied by hemorrhaging and by acute physical and moral pain.
>
> They are not subject to infection or decomposition, do not result in the death of any living tissue, do not emit any foul odors, do not change, do not form any scar tissue, and remain unchanged for years and years, against all biological laws of nature.[6]

In other words, the stigmata were real wounds. They bled and they hurt, yet they never destroyed tissue, they remained the same for long periods of time, and they did not leave scars. Padre Pio had not inflicted them on himself, nor were they the results of illness. They obviously had a supernatural dimension.

The World's Attention
Few outside of Italy knew of Padre Pio before World War II. Though his gifts were already manifesting themselves, his fame was mostly local. The remoteness of his monastery in a desolate mountainous region isolated him. How then did the world come to know of him?

One way was through photographs. Pio did not like to be photographed, although he was a physically attractive person with an expressive face and a beautiful smile. He let himself be photographed only because his superiors allowed it and because people told him the photos did good. Indeed, the photos seemed to exert a kind of spiritual power or charisma: Seeing Pio's picture drew many to his ministry.

A second way knowledge of Pio spread was through his spiritual children. This circle, especially the original group, brought many to Padre Pio through their stories, prayers and personal witness to what he could do for people.

One of them, John McCaffery, wrote, "Each person had to find his or her own San Giovanni." The town, the friary and the man were not only places on a map to which one could get; they were also destinations of a spiritual journey, an inward pilgrimage. The way to Padre Pio began, McCaffery wrote, "when you set out on your journey, for already you had begun to see things in a different perspective and to project yourself toward the great spiritual experience that awaited you." Pilgrims took the train or drove to Foggia, the nearest major town. "With arrival at Foggia you had the sensation of crossing a physical Rubicon and entering Padre Pio's territorial realm."[7]

One then drove up into the hills to the town of San Giovanni and the friary. "You'll find Padre Pio. You'll certainly find him!" said an Italian military officer to Katharina Tangari, who had asked about the padre.[8] Why? Because he was waiting for you.

"Up there," says McCaffery in describing what he felt as he approached San Giovanni, "was the greatest man in the world today, one of the most sublime saints the world had ever seen—aware of my arrival, as he was, I am convinced, of that of every single soul who came to see him there."[9]

The conviction that the padre knew you were coming, knew what you needed for the good of your soul and your life, was not simply a belief in his clairvoyance, though his supernatural knowledge often was confirmed for a pilgrim. It was also an expression of his concern for everyone who came to see him. He faced crowds every day, week after week, decade after decade. Yet, heroically and like the saint that he was, he cared about each individual. "Each person he knew was a soul to be saved, for each he was a father, an individual father."[10]

Mass with Padre Pio

The pilgrim's day began at 4:00 AM to allow time to rise and get to the friary church for Padre Pio's five o'clock Mass. Those who stayed in hotels remember the sound of phone after phone ringing four o'clock wake-up calls throughout the establishment.

Walking to the church would be a parade of pilgrims, and invariably a group was already waiting at the closed door in an attempt to get a good seat, as close as possible to the altar. When the doors opened, a commotion usually accompanied the rush of people into the church. This moment became somewhat legendary, in particular because of the behavior of *La Pie Donne,* the "pious ladies," about whom more will be said later.

A murmur would go up, "pleased and affectionate," when Padre Pio appeared to say Mass. He said the Latin Mass, and so "everyone felt at home, both Italians and foreigners."[11] Whatever the distractions the crowds or heat or cold caused, everyone followed the liturgy with the utmost attentiveness.

It was a unique and unforgettable experience. One woman said, "We really felt we were taking part in the sacrifice he offered on the altar. He used to glance at one of us, and then another, until everybody was included and had added his or her part to his own sublime performance."[12]

Many said they had never been part of another Mass like it. The way Padre Pio celebrated took people directly to the heart of the mystery. "I was completely, overwhelmingly mesmerized," said one man from England. "Here was Christ on the cross....You were really present at the Crucifixion....I'd *never* had this experience of witnessing Calvary. I was utterly overcome."[13]

Padre Pio's stigmata indicated how God had chosen him to participate in Christ's Passion in a special way. It is not surprising then that when Pio presided over the sacrifice of the Mass, he entered deeply into the meaning of the sacrament and let that meaning show forth to those gathered. The Eucharist makes Christ's sacrifice real for us here and now, and the priest acts *in persona Christi,* "in the person of Christ." Padre Pio's Mass made these beliefs real in ways most people had never before experienced.

> [He has] not a physical intensity, for his movements are slow and deliberate, his voice full and low-pitched, but an intensity of the spirit wherein we now glimpse a Padre Pio obviously inhabiting a world other than the material world around him; at times clearly suffering, at times as though looking on things unseen by us, at times in apparent mental converse; through all and above all his evident tremendous consciousness of the significance of his words and actions.[14]

Especially at the consecration of the bread and wine, "in the midst of a throng of worshipers now deadly silent and at the height of their concentration, one felt that truly this was the center of the universe. Wherever the sacrifice of the Mass is offered up, that is it. But here one realized it."[15]

What an irony, and one not lost on observers like John McCaffery: The center of the universe comes to "a remote, barren hillside, in a congregation largely made up of poor people, ignorant in the eyes of the world."[16]

After Mass, which usually lasted about ninety minutes, Padre Pio walked back to the sacristry to remove his vestments and make his thanksgiving. Even here people surrounded him, waiting for him to finish. Then, as he proceeded to go back to the monastery, people asked for his blessing, requested something from him, kissed his hand or touched his garments. At the end of this walk he would turn to face everyone, give a general blessing and wish all *"Buona giornata!"* a greeting the people returned.[17]

Thus began Padre Pio's public day.

The Confessor

Not much later the padre came back to the church for confession, another pillar of his ministry. In fifty-one years it is estimated that Padre Pio heard two million confessions. From 1918 until 1923, when his superiors reduced the time he was available for confessions, he sat in the confessional from fifteen to nineteen hours a day. In the 1940s and 1950s he heard confessions between five and eight hours a day: women in the morning in the church's open confessional, men face-to-face in the sacristy, "often with his hands on their shoulders."[18]

As more and more people came to confess to him, it became necessary to make a schedule. A person who signed up for confession frequently had to wait anywhere from a day to a week. Making a confession to Padre Pio was the main reason many people came to San Giovanni. Such was the atmosphere that many "wanted to be in the church just to be near Padre Pio while confessions were going on."[19]

Padre Pio first asked a penitent the standard question of how long it had been since his or her last confession. This routine exchange seemed to establish a spiritual link between Pio and the penitent, because after it, as pilgrim Katharina Tangari wrote, "it suddenly seemed as if Padre Pio knew everything about us." If you were vague, he got to the point. "We would get the feeling that Padre Pio knew us, that his eye could see our soul as it really was before God."[20]

In the confessional Padre Pio was all things to all people. "Where tenderness was needed, it flowed out from him. Where help and prompting were required, they were given. Where bracing and strengthening were called for, they were provided."[21]

On rare occasions Padre Pio could be harsh, saying something devastating to a penitent and even kicking the person out of the confessional. He was not merely losing his temper. His wrath came in response to "insincerity, hypocrisy, or falsehood," and in many cases "the penitent would be found later to have returned in more correct or chastened dispositions and would be received accordingly."[22]

In response to someone who came to him with a family problem she felt to be unbearable, Pio replied, "And you really can't bear this?"[23] To a woman who hadn't been to church since her husband's death, Pio said, "Because you lost your husband, you also lost God? Go away! Go away!" and slid shut the confessional window on her.[24]

Pio had no patience for those who concealed the truth from him, tried to test him or wanted an experience of celebrity, and he saw through these pretenses. He often "realized that their motives or pleas were superstitious or purely material and egotistical, or that they were treating him like some witch doctor or medicine man and had little thought of reforming their lives."[25]

If someone wanted only to manipulate him—in other words, to focus on what *he* could give them rather than on what God could do through him—they were in for a rough surprise. A well-known political figure's visit occasioned this remark from the padre: "Well, well! How the world has changed since I was young! In those days the police were to be found at the heels of thieves and robbers. Now they go before them on motorcycles to clear the way!"[26]

The Italian comedic actor Carlo Campanini recounts that an Italian organized crime figure came to San Giovanni to have Padre Pio hear his confession. Given his exalted status back in Naples—he thought of himself as *Il Commendatore*—this man thought he deserved to go ahead of those who had been waiting. "Everybody is a *commendatore* here," said Campanini, a friend of Padre Pio. "He'll just have to take his turn."

When the criminal entered the confessional, his knees had not hit the ground when he made a great noise and came out of the confessional "like a bullet from a gun!" as Campanini described it. "He did not give me time to say a word," the man said, "but straightaway called me an old pig and told me to get out!"

"Well," Campanini said, "you must know more about why he called you that than I. He certainly had his own good reasons."

"I can't think why," the man said, "unless it is because I happen to be living with a woman who is not my wife."

"It just could be that," Campanini commented.[27]

A Heart of Love

Padre Pio gave another reason for his occasional gruffness: "I act like that so that I don't let myself be overcome with emotion. Seeing people suffer is enough to bring me to tears, and then I would no longer be able to continue my ministry."[28]

Whether provoking people to sincerity or covering for his emotions, Padre Pio's harshness grew out of compassion. "It's true," Pio's follower Giuseppe Canaponi said, "that at times Padre Pio would raise his voice with people in confession and scold them. But he did it...for their conversion....When he would speak about the sick and their suffering, his eyes would well up with tears. Sometimes he was so moved that he couldn't speak. Often he would hide his feelings...to the point that he would appear rather sullen. But this was only a defense mechanism."[29]

Said his friend the journalist and radio personality and producer Giovanni Gigliozzi, "I can truly say that I haven't known anyone who was capable of so much tenderness."[30]

According to Katharine Tangari, Padre Pio did not see his role as confessor to be consoling or comforting. What he did was inspire courage and strength to face the challenges and troubles of life. "He often took from us the pains we had brought with us into his confessional....The same cross that had seemed too heavy for our strength became, with his words and his example, light and quite bearable."[31]

Pio would not let his penitents be sad or discouraged; he tolerated no despair. He recommended prayer and "exhorted us to trust in God and in Divine Providence."[32] "His mission on earth," wrote the Duchess of St. Albans, "was not to patch up broken hearts but to reclaim lost souls and repentant sinners."[33] People "came away [from confession] not only cleansed," McCaffery writes, "but, in the sensing of his remoteness from sin and why, more keenly aware of what sin really meant."[34]

Padre Pio himself saw how repentance involved not only the fact of one's sins forgiven but the gaining of an awareness of sin and a desire to avoid it in the future. "I believe that not a great number of souls go to hell," he said. "God loves us so much. He formed us in His image. God the Son incarnate died to redeem us....And it is my belief that even when we have passed from the consciousness of this world, when we appear to be dead, God, before He judges us, will give us a chance to see and understand what sin really is. And if we understand it properly, how could we fail to repent?"[35]

Lessons from Padre Pio
At around 10:00 in the morning Padre Pio distributed Communion to those who wanted to receive it from him. After Communion the men met him in the sacristy for another opportunity to receive a blessing or an exhortation. In the afternoon he celebrated Benediction of the Blessed Sacrament, which followed the rosary and now and then a homily from a guest Capuchin preacher. Some days Pio presided at baptisms.

Because he was also spiritual director of the friars, Pio needed to take time for these responsibilities as well. Always—whether he was in the sacristy, leaving the confessional or going back and forth between the church and the friary—people pressed him for a brief word or a blessing on themselves, their children or a religious object. He tried "above all to see and speak with as many as possible of those hosts of people who [had] come from far and near to receive comfort from him."[36]

Given the large numbers of those waiting to see him,

he had to keep his words short and effective. But his brevity was also part of his gift. He concentrated on the essentials, and his words "could strike the heart profoundly and could shake up consciences in a surprising manner."[37]

Perhaps the greatest grace of confession and other encounters with Padre Pio was a deeper appreciation of the religious truths behind them. For all of Pio's spiritual power, what he did pointed to God, who was behind it all. In the same way Brother André gave all credit to God and Saint Joseph, and Solanus Casey insisted it was God's will, not his, that people who talked with him found healing.

The Capuchin Padre Gian Antonio spoke of his first confession with Padre Pio, when both were young men. When Gian came out, he was elated. "'Why are you so happy?' I asked myself. 'Because you have been confessed by Padre Pio? Why, certainly, he was an admirable confessor and gave you excellent counsel. But you have been to other good confessors before and received much similar good advice. The fact of the matter is that you should be walking on air, not merely now, but *each* time that you come out from confession!' And that was Padre Pio's first little lesson for me."[38]

At the end of the day Padre Pio joined the community for night prayer. Before going to his room, he went to his superior for a blessing, then visited with his best friend, Padre Agostino. Most nights Pio prayed and read Scripture until 1:00 AM or later, completing his twenty-hour day and giving himself a few short hours of sleep before he started all over again with early morning Mass.

Where Is Padre Pio?

One of the more fantastic gifts Padre Pio shared with other Franciscan saints was the ability to be in more than one place at the same time, known as bilocation.

Once some of the friars attended a concert at the monastery. During the intermission Pio put his head down on his arms, resting on the back of the chair in front of him, and he remained in this position for a few moments. The others thought he was tired and let him be. When the concert resumed, Pio lifted his head and continued enjoying the performance.

Now, the only times Padre Pio left the monastery were to go into town once a year to vote and, in later years, to visit the hospital. So imagine the surprise when a family told the monastery's superior how delighted they were that Padre Pio had paid a visit to their ailing loved one and how much better the man was feeling.

"But," Padre Carmelo said, "Padre Pio didn't come into the village yesterday evening." When the family insisted that Pio had indeed been at their house, Padre Carmelo asked when the visit had occurred, though "he already knew the answer. It was at the time of the concert interval."[39]

The broadcaster Giovanni Gigliozzi, one of Padre Pio's close friends, suffered from migraine headaches. One headache came upon him right before a broadcast, and he told the director he could not go on. The panic-stricken director told Giovanni to go lie down and see if he might feel better. This Gigliozzi did, though he knew it wouldn't help. He was not thinking at all of Padre Pio.

While lying down, he heard noises and opened his

eyes to see none other than the padre standing by the couch. Smiling, Pio laid his hand on Giovanni's head, then vanished, as did the headache. Taking a moment to gather himself, Giovanni then proceeded to broadcast his program.

The following Sunday he went to San Giovanni. When he saw Padre Pio, he knelt down and kissed the hand of the padre, who asked, "Well, Giovanni, and how is the head?" to which Gigliozzi replied, "Thank you, Padre, very well indeed." "Ah," said Padre Pio with a smile, "these hallucinations!"[40]

Knowing God's Mind

A number of stories testify to Pio's ability to know things he could not have known without supernatural inspiration. This kind of knowledge always served a constructive purpose. What he knew was a piece of information key to a person's spiritual needs.

A recurring story has to do with Pio's occasional listing of a penitent's sins before the person had the chance to say anything. One confession began with the padre saying, "I will do the talking." He sometimes reminded penitents if anything were left out.

This was a gift he shared with the other doorkeepers. One of Brother André's biographers reported: "Some people who came out of his office were surprised to find that Brother André had spoken to them as if he knew their past. Brother André corrected things, saying, 'But didn't such a thing happen like this?' And the people involved were forced to note that this was indeed the case!"[41]

On occasion Father Solanus told people what they

were going to do with their lives. When a seminary student worried that his stomach problems would prevent his becoming a priest, Solanus told him that he would become a priest of longstanding. This man later retired after fifty years in the priesthood. To a woman who planned to become a nun, Solanus said she would marry a man who would become a policeman, and the couple would have several children. The woman married a soldier who later became a police officer; they had eight children.

At times the doorkeepers could foresee whether a sick person would recover or would die. During the polio epidemic of the 1930s, Solanus's prayer helped to heal many a sick child. One father, whose son was about to go into the hospital with the disease, called Solanus, who enrolled the child in the SMA and told the father, "Don't worry. The boy will be all right tomorrow." And a surprised doctor indeed confirmed the recovery that night.[42]

Someone said, "One had a way of knowing by the way Father Solanus spoke whether he would promise a cure, or whether he just asked us to accept God's will." Brother Ignatius Milne observed, "To those people for whom he gave...specific and detailed instructions, their problems were solved whatever they might have been. For those for whom Father merely said, 'I will pray for them,' they were not."[43]

André told a young man with tuberculosis, "You're going to die tomorrow. The Good God wants you with Him." When the man said he had a wife and young children, André told him that Saint Joseph would look after the family. "Your death," he added, "will be sweet and calm." The next day the man died in peace.[44]

Padre Pio observers noted that when he promised to pray in response to a request, chances were good that the prayer would be answered. But if he advised someone to pray for whatever God saw best, this meant, be prepared to accept the prayer not being answered.

One may wonder at such "bedside manners." But the bluntness of the doorkeepers reflects something deeper than simple honesty. André, Solanus and Pio wanted at all times to draw those they spoke with into a relationship of faith. Whether the prospect was recovery or imminent death, they invited people to trust in the loving care of God for themselves and their loved ones. Take this step into faith, they were saying—whether by promising to pray, be anointed, do a good work, participate more in the sacraments, join a Mass association or prepare for death—and God will respond to you with healing, reassurance, a resolution of your problems or a peaceful death.

Sanctity's Aroma

Another special gift that Padre Pio bore was "the perfume." When the holiness of a person is so great as to be almost palpable, we say they bear "the odor of sanctity." For the friends of Padre Pio, a real smell of perfume signaled his presence. While miraculous in itself, this odor was not so much a dramatic event as a gentle reminder of Pio's encouragement and approval of his spiritual children.

A great variety of people have told of the perfume. John McCaffery's story comes in the context of arriving early to get a good view of Padre Pio's morning Mass. While he was waiting, another Capuchin, Padre Vincenzo, came out to say Mass at a side altar. Vincenzo had no one to serve the Mass, and when he came to the words of consecration, McCaffery wondered whether he should help.

McCaffery then smelled the perfume, an overwhelming scent that seemed to come out of nowhere, and its message was clear to him. He went to serve Padre Vincenzo's Mass, thereby missing the Mass of Padre Pio. "It was the most fantastic pat on the head or back I have ever received," he wrote, "a proof that, if I was unable to follow Padre Pio's Mass, my own puny sacrifice had been duly followed by him."[45]

CHAPTER SEVEN

Healing Faith

*If we could only learn to appreciate the holy faith and
the innumerable blessings flowing from it and the
blessings otherwise surrounding us; we could
never have time to worry about anything,
except that we're so little appreciative.*

—Solanus Casey

In the Gospels healing and faith are intimately connected. Sometimes faith leads to healing; other times people come to faith because a healing occurs. Whatever the particular situation, faith and healing are two sides of the same coin.

Obviously, Christians believe in a God who wills their salvation, healing and wholeness, but the question becomes what form that salvation will take. André was as much or even more interested in people's souls—in their faith—than in their physical health. Sometimes the physical condition symbolized the spiritual condition. Joseph Pichette testified, "Brother André told me that some people were not healed because they…did not pray enough or that they would not adequately follow the rules of Christian morality."[1]

The purpose of André's work was not simply healing. If it were, everyone who sought him out would have found healing, and not all did. What did happen was an act of faith that opened the sufferer to the actions of God.

When there was no healing, the reason might be a poor disposition on the part of the petitioner, but it might also be that God did not will the person's healing in the way it was requested. To his elderly cousin who had lost her sight, Brother André said, "You have enough faith to bear this infirmity. You must endure it for the love of God. It's your vocation."[2]

Joseph Pichette recalls André's telling people on occasion, "It is better to suffer." He also once said, "I can't obtain the cure of certain sick persons because the eternal salvation of these persons is attached to their infirmity. But people don't understand this."[3]

One of his colleagues observed, "Those who are healed quickly are either those who do not have faith or those who have little faith—so that they might have faith; while those who already have a firm faith are not healed quickly, since the Good God would rather test them and make them suffer in order to sanctify them more."[4]

André said the same thing in so many words: "Those who suffer something have something to offer God.... And when they manage to endure successfully, that is a miracle that keeps repeating."[5]

Receiving God's Gifts

For Solanus, too, healing was never separate from an active faith. Michael Crosby writes, "In Solanus's mind, the healings took place because the people requesting them promised to do three things: (1) believe, (2) pray with faith, and (3) make a promise."[6] Speaking of the afflicted, Solanus said, "If God wishes to cure them, they will be cured if they have faith."[7]

Faith brought people to Solanus, and he directed them to enter more deeply into their faith. But for him faith was something deeper still: realizing the goodness and presence of God and responding to it. "If we could only learn to appreciate the holy faith and the innumerable blessings flowing from it and the blessings otherwise surrounding us," he wrote, "we could never have time to worry about anything, except that we're so little appreciative."[8]

On another occasion he wrote, "We are continually immersed in God's merciful graces like the air that permeates us." In this environment, each person has work to do: "participation and cooperation in [God's] own divine activity."[9]

Belief in God, Solanus thought, was the only position a rational person could take. It was irrational, in his mind, to look at creation and see anything else. Everything is a gift from God that invites us to participate in God's work in creation. In this way, for Solanus, all things the church offered were a means of grace. Faith was a total reality, lived and experienced through the church.

Religion, for Solanus, was "the unrecognized science,"[10] and much of faith and religion had to do with confidence in God and trust in his divine providence. We are to accept God's will, whatever happens. "Blessed be God in all His designs"[11] was his statement of radical acceptance as well as an act of gratitude and faith.

Solanus had an unconditional trust in God and a belief that good would come out of any situation. He constantly reminded others to have that same confidence. With trust in God comes not only acceptance but also gratitude for what God does. Ingratitude, Solanus said, breaks our relationships with God and others, while the greatest "science of all times," he believed, was "the science of our happy relationship with God and our neighbor."[12]

Many times people use the expression "It's God's will" to explain events, usually bad ones. Solanus, however, believed in God's will in a radical way that went beyond easy explanations. Acceptance of the will of God, in the good and the bad, gave him—and those with similar faith—peace, assuredness and spiritual power. It made for a life of gratitude and simplicity, and it contributed to the building up of what Solanus thought to be each person's destiny: happy relationships with God and neighbor.

Ultimately, the way of believing Solanus promoted was a way of living at one with God. And he became an instrument of God's presence. One person remarked, "He made you feel the presence of God in your life. He is the only one in my life who made me feel that way."[13]

A Fact of Faith

Padre Pio as well saw healing to be part of faith. He knew he could not *give* people faith, but he also knew what faith could do. He once said, "I am able to be a humble instrument in the hands of God, but I have not the ability to give you the gift of the true faith. This, in fact, is a gift that can only be given by God. Therefore, I will pray that God will grant you the gift of faith; that is, namely, that you will believe that Jesus Christ is the Messiah."[14] Someone observed of Padre Pio, "when people were in good faith, he always found a way of reaching them."[15]

One of the padre's spiritual daughters, Katharina Tangari, wrote:

> Receiving the grace of having our prayers heard is a fact of faith that always moves us insofar as it shows us, in a very special way, the loving intervention of Divine Providence in our lives....We do not know beforehand the ways and conditions....How then can we receive [knowledge of the way]? Through faith, through our humble and at the same time daring attempt to draw down upon us God's mercy and providence. God has sewn a desire into our heart, and we begin to pray so that it may be heard. Often, however, we see that our own prayers are not enough; it seems that our own strength is not enough to carry our prayers to Heaven....So we look for somebody who can help us.[16]

The doorkeepers proved to be the "somebody" for millions.

Part Three
HOLY WORKS

CHAPTER EIGHT

Works of Mercy

I have two loves, the sick and the poor.

—Solanus Casey

The majority of French Canadians of Brother André's time, especially early in his life, were people of humble means. Apart from the business and professional elites and a small middle class, French Canadians farmed, worked in factories, ran small businesses or were public servants. Wages were low, hours long, few public welfare programs existed and many workers had large families to support. Few had educations beyond primary school.[1]

Long before liberation theology Brother André had a preferential option for the poor. "He loved the poor and welcomed them with even more sympathy than he did wealthier people," said his friend Joseph Pichette. "When I first met Brother André, I was poor and it seems he took better care of me in those days than when I began to earn some money."[2]

Sometimes the plight of those who came to Brother André moved him to tears. He always spoke to people about God, encouraged them to pray and had advice for them. "Having frequented the Oratory for thirty years," Pichette said, "I must have seen hundreds of healings, perhaps even a thousand....I can attest to having brought many people to the Oratory and that all, though not all were cured, came back satisfied."[3]

The doorkeepers all had the gift of being able to relate to anyone, and like Jesus, they had a special relationship with the poor. Working people made up a large number of their visitors. These must have seen in the doorkeeper someone they could approach; after all, the three had come from rural and small-town backgrounds and knew what it was like to work for a living.

They all liked being with people. Their reputations for sanctity never stood in the way of their everyday relationships. In the doorkeepers the divine became accessible in an especially direct way, and it should not be surprising that they mirrored that accessibility to those around them.

The ability of people to identify with the doorkeepers, and vice versa, also has a spiritual dimension. John McCaffery wrote, "Like the church, [Padre Pio] was and is there chiefly for those who need help and guidance, rather than for those who don't. And in order to help, he had to be close to us, to be able to fully understand us and our difficulties."[4]

Padre Pio, McCaffery said, was "definitely one of us."[5] He welcomed everyone, even the powerful and rich if they came to him with sincere hearts. Adds Renzo Allegri, one of his biographers, "Padre Pio loved people.

He wept and suffered with those who were afflicted, yet he laughed with those who were happy."[6]

But the vast majority of those who sought him out were poor, and Padre Pio saw in them the "suffering brethren of Christ and loved them the more for that."[7]

Father Solanus was a "real person," someone to whom others could relate. He enjoyed mingling at parish picnics and eating the hot dogs (with onions) served there. He was not above stopping for a beer at a tavern that one of his benefactors operated. He played billiards and baseball and was a Detroit Tigers fan. At the age of eighty he joined in games of volleyball and tennis. Ahead of his time, he promoted healthy eating (except for the hot dogs), and he liked to jog to keep trim.

Social Action

The doorkeepers' compassion extended beyond personal connections with individuals to social concerns. "If we are to be considered children of God, we must pursue justice and peace," Solanus said.[8] He once wrote in a letter, "What a marvelously different society we would have here, and what an ideal world to live in if we all would keep in mind the assurance of Jesus, 'What you have done to the least of my brethren, you have done to me.'"[9]

Solanus visited the sick in homes and hospitals at all hours of the day and night, and he visited the families of those who had died. Starting with his days in Yonkers, he gave away food to those who needed it, sometimes sacrificing his own meals or raiding the friary's kitchen. When another Capuchin objected to the latter practice, Solanus said, "As long as there is one hungry person, this food does not belong to us."[10]

He was instrumental in establishing a soup kitchen in Detroit. For years the Capuchins there had given food to the hungry who came to their door, but during the Depression as many as 150 people came each day to ask for something to eat. In response to this need, Solanus led the effort to set up a soup kitchen in the community's hall. It was one of the first in Detroit and eventually served up to three thousand people daily. Today the Capuchins at St. Bonaventure's continue to serve around fifty thousand meals a month and provide clothing and furniture to those who need them.

Solanus helped stock the soup kitchen by asking bakeries and butchers to donate food and making trips to the countryside to pick up provisions. When supplies ran short, Solanus's penchant for the miraculous spilled over into feeding the hungry. One man shared about the day when there was no bread on hand and about three hundred men were waiting to eat:

> [Solanus] went over to the hall and told the men who were waiting in line, "Just wait and God will provide." Father Solanus said an "Our Father" after inviting the men to join him in the prayer. We just turned around and opened the front door to go out, and there was a bakery man coming with a big basket full of food. He had his whole truck full of stuff, and he proceeded to unload it. When the men saw this they started to cry and tears were running down their cheeks. Father Solanus, in his simple way, said, "See, God provides. Nobody will starve as long as you put your confidence in God, in Divine Providence."[11]

On the occasion of a benefit celebration for the soup kitchen in 1937, Solanus gave a radio address to the people of Detroit. In his brief remarks he thanked the benefactors who helped to make the soup kitchen possible, and he also spoke of the poor the Capuchins served: "We admit that we have tried to be of service to the poorest of the poor, but must add that it was simple duty....Our lot has been cast among the simple lives of the poor, and our object is to give them spiritual aid and, if possible, material help as well."[12]

Power Politics

Solanus and Pio took a keen interest in social and political issues, while Brother André was about as apolitical as one could be. Apparently he never read the newspapers or listened to the radio. He claimed in 1936 to know nothing about Hitler, Mussolini or Franklin Roosevelt.[13]

Solanus had a passionate concern for the plight of Ireland and wrote letters to the Irish-American press. Pio was an active citizen, voting Christian Democratic, as did many of the friars, and encouraging his followers to do the same. When a plebiscite abolished the Italian monarchy, Pio was not displeased; he had come to believe that the Italian royal family lacked faith.[14]

In 1919 an economic downturn brought on intense labor conflicts in Italy, which the burgeoning Socialist-Fascist political duel exacerbated. San Giovanni Rotondo was not immune, and the 1920 municipal election threatened violence to such a degree that the authorities assigned about 120 soldiers and *carabinieri* (state police) to San Giovanni. A riot in October killed fifteen people and injured over eighty.

The mayor, Francesco Morcaldi, went to the friary for advice. Padre Pio had earlier told him to "go into the countryside and calm people down." This time Pio told Morcaldi, "Reconcile, my son, reconcile." A few days later he proposed to the mayor a program to improve working conditions, educate laborers, assist war orphans and improve hospital facilities and the road, sanitation and telephone systems.[15]

Even at this early date we see how Pio was interested in the welfare of the people and had ideas for developing San Giovanni from a poor, underserved town to a modern municipality. The pilgrims he attracted helped speed this modernization, as did the hospital he would build.

Padre Pio's Hospital

It is one thing to consider how Padre Pio, living in an out-of-the-way place, became one of the great saints of all time. It is just as miraculous to ponder how another major part of his ministry and legacy came to be: *La Casa Sollievo della Sofferenza*, the House for the Relief of Suffering.

John McCaffery puts it: "If one thinks just for a moment of what is implied in the setting up of a modern four-hundred-bed hospital, the immensity and complexity of the task are evident. Situate it then in the middle of nowhere; make all its prodigious running costs depend upon more or less haphazard charitable donations; consider that it was so constructed as to be capable of harmonious expansion to its present [1978] number of a thousand beds."[16]

Padre Pio started with an idea, a plot of land and a small group of devoted helpers. Incorporation of the

Casa occurred in October 1946. Friends and collaborators of Padre Pio made up the first shareholders. Pio tabbed his friend Giuseppe Orlando to be the first director of the existing-in-name-only hospital.

Giuseppe asked him, "But, Piuccio, why do I have to make them laugh behind my back and yours? Start work for a big clinic without a drawing, without a design, without an engineer?"

The padre replied, "You must start the work."[17] With the eccentric Angelo Lupi as builder and architect, the group employed farm workers to clear the land and build.

After ten years of fundraising, construction and recruitment of personnel, the hospital's dedication day, May 5, 1956, finally arrived. Addressing the crowd of some fifteen thousand, Padre Pio thanked the hospital's benefactors with words that summarized his spirituality: "This work which you see today is only starting out on its life, but this creation, to grow and become adult, needs and asks for your generosity so that it may become a hospital city, technically adapted to the most demanding needs and also to the disciplined order demanded by militant Franciscanism, a place of prayer and science, where human beings can be united in Christ Crucified, as a single flock with a single shepherd."

To the doctors he said, "Bring God to the sick. It will be more valuable than any other treatment....You have the mission of curing the sick, but if at the patient's bedside you do not bring the warmth of loving care, I fear that medicine will not be of much use."[18]

The *Casa* boasted two operating rooms and departments of general surgery, urology, cardiology, orthopedics, trauma, pediatrics, obstetrics, radiology and physical therapy, as well as laboratories for clinical research and an outpatient clinic. The *Casa* was "one of the most beautiful as well as one of the most modern and fully-equipped hospitals in the world. It even has a helicopter landing place on the roof for emergency patients," according to the *New York Times*.[19]

The building was air-conditioned—a rarity in Italy for years to come. Padre Pio, criticized for allowing too much to be spent on luxuries, answered, "Nothing is too good or too beautiful for the sick and suffering!"[20]

The opening of a state-of-the-art medical facility, providing free care in a remote region and founded by a Capuchin friar, brought attention to Padre Pio and his ministry, especially in Italy. The influx of hospital personnel and visitors, plus more people seeking to visit the padre, brought more change to the little town. "New houses sprang up for the doctors. Shops came into being to cater to all these extra customers, more hotels were built and even the roads were mended! Prosperity came to San Giovanni, up to a point."[21]

Padre Pio and the *Casa* put San Giovanni on the map, so to speak. Even the modest old monastery was not immune from progress. To accommodate the greater number of pilgrims, the Capuchins eventually built a new and larger friary church.

Since Padre Pio's death the hospital has tripled in size. It is now regarded as one of the best hospitals in Europe. The facility Padre Pio established for handicapped children has grown as well, and an outpatient clinic and retirement home have opened. God used this holy man to build his kingdom in more ways than one!

CHAPTER NINE

The Oratory of Saint Joseph

*There are, most certainly, extraordinary events
taking place here…and greater wonders
than the healing of the body.*

—Archbishop Bruchési of Montréal, November 17, 1912

Padre Pio was not the only builder among the door-keepers. While his project came from his concern for the sick and poor, Brother André's arose from his devotion to Saint Joseph.

Brother André's superiors turned him down flat when he first asked to build a chapel in honor of Saint Joseph. He accepted the decision out of obedience and did not protest, but he had other means of obtaining what he wanted.

First André began a quiet supernatural campaign. He walked on the mountain in the evenings, sometimes by himself, sometimes with others, and as he went he cleared paths, scattered medals of Saint Joseph and prayed. When one of his religious brothers came to fetch him one day for supper, he said, "I can't leave. Saint Joseph wants me to promise him to build his chapel."[1]

André turned the small statue of Saint Joseph in his room to face the mountain. Saint Joseph seemed to be pleased to be looking that way. Brother Aldéric told André that the statue of the saint in his room was always turned to face the mountain, even when Aldéric turned it to face away from the window before he left his room. André noted, "That's because Saint Joseph wants to be honored there."[2]

Brother Aldéric and others shared in André's methods of prayer. A few years later, when the owner of the land on which the oratory would be built resisted selling the parcel to Holy Cross, Brother Aldéric and Father Louis Geoffrion hiked up to the top of the property and buried a medal of Saint Joseph by a tree. Not long after, the landowner relented, and on July 22, 1896, Father Geoffrion signed the deed for the land.

But not all of André's efforts relied on prayer. One time when he was ill in the community infirmary, his bed was next to one occupied by the college's superior, Father Lecavalier, Geoffrion's successor. In the course of his infirmary stay, Brother André managed to get permission from the superior to build a chapel on the mountain.

Starting Small

Father Lecavalier chose a site for the first chapel, but Brother André wanted another spot, saying he had "seen" the oratory in that location. At the blessing of the enlarged chapel in 1912, André made it clear, however, that his idea for a place of prayer to Saint Joseph did not come to him in a supernatural vision but expressed his devotion to the saint.

"Do you believe that you've had a vision? Did St. Joseph speak to you?" someone asked.

"There has been nothing of the kind," André said. "I have nothing but devotion to St. Joseph. That alone is what guides me and gives me utter confidence in the project."[3]

How to go about raising the money for even a small chapel? André had begun saving money for the chapel's construction, with permission, by putting aside the five cents per haircut he earned as the community barber. But savings he built up in those increments was not going to build much.

Private donors provided the bulk of the need, but these were not the rich. When the main oratory began to go up, Father Émile Deguire, later a rector of the oratory and a close friend and confidant of Brother André, said, "Until now, contrary to popular rumor, we have not received any major donations. What has been built so far is due more to the offerings of the poor than to the grants of the rich."[4] A fitting source of funds, given the fact that André was of the poor, and it was they whom he most loved to serve.

Brother André started looking for building materials and help. His main collaborator was Brother Abundius Piché, a cabinet-maker and the college carpenter, who designed the chapel and did the actual building. Other volunteers joined, and this group, using less-than-ideal tools, began by clearing land and making a path through the woods to the chapel site.

Another helper came from the ranks of the sick. Brother André visited Calixte Richard, a master mason who was suffering from stomach cancer. In his characteristic way André told him, "You're not sick!" and instructed Richard's wife to give the man some soup, though he had not eaten in some time. He led Richard to the table and asked him, "Should Saint Joseph heal you, would you come and help me build a chapel on the mountain?"

When the astonished Richard said yes, André replied, "I'll see you in the morning then." Richard was there first thing in the morning, and he worked without pain. He eventually brought several other men to help.[5]

From the first clearing of land to the completion of the building, the project took almost three months, but the actual construction of the small building did not take long, "seven or eight days...on our free time," according to Brother Abundius. "Brother André was convinced the chapel would eventually have to be enlarged, but he was still happy with the modest beginnings."[6]

The original chapel of Saint Joseph on Mount Royal was indeed small: only eighteen feet by sixteen feet and twenty-five feet tall with a capacity of ten people. The front of the building consisted of large doors that swung open, so more worshipers could attend open-air Masses.

Brother Abundius used spruce for the building. For the altar, which took more time to carve and which he installed later, during the winter of 1906, he used pine. The *Annals of Saint Joseph*, one of the oratory's publications, described the altar a few years later as "a lovely sculpted piece incorporating, in its centre, a large niche showcasing the statue of the Holy Patriarch, as well as two smaller ones, each displaying a censer-bearing angel."[7]

On the day of the chapel's dedication, October 19, 1904, hundreds of people gathered, including Monsignor Zotique Racicot, vicar general of the diocese of Montréal. *La Presse,* the major Montréal newspaper, reported on the opening of the chapel: "From the tramway line, one can see the modest building, nestled like a little hermitage in a cluster of birches and pine trees. The cross on top of the roof is fifteen feet high, and can be spotted easily over the treetops....This chapel, dedicated to Saint Joseph, will be unique in its kind in Canada. Pilgrims will travel here from all parts of the country to venerate the saint, and to plead for his intercession."[8]

For the first five years of its life, the ownership and management of the oratory was in the hands of lay-people, friends of Brother André, who worked in collaboration with Holy Cross and the Montréal bishop. Only in 1909 did Holy Cross assume responsibility for the oratory and, a year later, assign to it a chaplain, Father Adolphe Clément, himself a close and lifelong friend of Brother André.

A Movement of Piety

By 1909 the number of André's tasks had been diminishing as he devoted more and more time to his healing ministry, and in this year Holy Cross officially named him guardian of the oratory and told him he no longer had to do the work of porter, which he had done for almost forty years. But he remained a "spiritual doorkeeper" in his work at the oratory and in his ministry to the afflicted.

In the fall of 1910 construction began on a new building to house the priests, brothers and sisters who worked at the college. When it was finished in 1915, the college and the oratory became separate entities. Another small building went up adjacent to the new rectory; this housed Brother André's office and a gift shop.

With the enlargement of the chapel in 1912, André moved to a room above the sanctuary. While simple, it was probably the best accommodations in which he had ever lived. The room even had electric lights. When the rectory was completed, André received a room there with the rest of the community, but he would occasionally use the room over the chapel to keep vigils with the afflicted.

At the dedication of the enlarged chapel on November 17, 1912, Archbishop Bruschési of Montréal said,

At this Oratory, Saint Joseph shall be honored in a special way, as is the Holy Virgin at Lourdes and Loreto. I see here the unfolding of a movement of piety....In the very beginning, a pious man put up a statue in this place. Every day, people came here to pray. Before long, a small chapel was built. But as those good people devoted to Saint Joseph arrived here in ever-larger numbers, it was necessary to enlarge it on more than one occasion. Work has just begun here, and I can foresee, in a not too distant future, the construction on the Mount Royal of a basilica worthy of Saint Joseph....

Might I say miracles are happening here? If I were to deny it, all these instruments [crutches and other items

> the healed had discarded], silent witnesses to so much suffering, would speak in my place....There are, most certainly, extraordinary events taking place here…and greater wonders than the healing of the body.[9]

One can see from this speech how even at this fairly early point in the oratory's history, the significance of what was happening on Mount Royal was already evident. Many visitors came every year, and in 1910 the oratory received almost twenty-five thousand letters, of which over a hundred talked about complete recoveries, forty-three hundred improvements in conditions and a little over three hundred other favors obtained.[10]

Raising Funds

Plans were afoot for a new main oratory, a building 325 feet long by 192 feet wide and 467 feet high. It would accommodate four thousand people seated, nine thousand standing. Estimated cost was $2.8 million, a colossal sum for the time. Brother André would play a significant part in God's provision.

Twice a year Brother André took a trip to New England. The journeys were supposed to be vacations, but his work followed him. He visited relatives, friends and priests he knew, and he frequently ended up ministering to the people who came to see him in homes, in parishes where he was staying and in hospitals. Though he usually showed up unannounced at the homes of family members, "He wasn't in the door one hour," a grandnephew said, "before there were 100 people outside the door. I still don't understand how they knew. We never understood."[11]

In some places the crowds were not a mystery: His hosts had put ads in the newspapers or on the radio about his upcoming visit. Sometimes these crowds put off Brother André. "What's this?" he once asked when he arrived at a home only to face a line of people snaking down the street. "I can't see them all! I came here to rest!" If people became demanding, he could get "a little rough."[12]

Brother André preferred traveling by car, even over great distances, because it allowed him a little privacy and prevented scenes on trains when people recognized him. He encouraged fast driving to save time and did not believe in making many stops, except to pray in churches.

Nor did he care about the condition of the vehicle. "So long as it has four wheels and runs, it's enough for me," he said.[13] Like Solanus, he frequently required his driver to pray with him during car trips. Other times he read the Bible or one of his devotional books or took a nap.

He carried in his bag and handed out Saint Joseph medals. From these trips he brought back crutches, canes and other devices that the healed no longer needed.

He also brought back bags full of cash and checks for the oratory. Just as when he accepted money in Montréal, he immediately gave the funds to his superiors. He "was never so happy as when he brought a large donation to his Superiors," said a professor who knew him.[14]

Age did not deter Brother André. When he was ninety he traveled to New York City to solicit a donation from John D. Rockefeller. What possessed André to entertain this notion is unclear; apparently he liked the idea because he had not thought of it before. While he never did get a personal interview with John D., who was also in his nineties, he did come back with the biggest check of the year from the first secretary of the Rockefeller Foundation.

The blessing of the new oratory's cornerstone took place on August 31, 1924, the three hundredth anniversary of Canada's consecration to Saint Joseph. The spirit of the saint was also present in the person of Monsignor Pietro di Maria, the Vatican's apostolic delegate to Canada, who oversaw the blessing and who also had a great devotion to Saint Joseph.[15]

A Place of Mercy

Go to the oratory today and you will see people praying for their needs and those of others. Maybe they are out of work and have come to pray to Saint Joseph the worker. Maybe they are sick or have a loved one who is sick. Whatever their reasons, in Brother André they feel close to the healing and counseling power of God.

Much as the doorkeepers attracted and were open to dealing with people of all faiths during their lifetimes, the institutions they left behind have become ecumenical places of prayer. Canadian Father Jules Beaulac, a frequent visitor to the oratory, wrote in 2004: "People of every nation, colour, age, health and, possibly, of various religions assemble to pray to God in the Eucharist, to Saint Joseph in the large Votive Chapel, and to Brother André at his tomb. The universal Church is truly present here and the salvation that Jesus brought to all is clearly manifested."[16]

"Many pilgrims can bear witness to the numerous favours granted by Saint Joseph," wrote Father

Jean-Pierre Aumont, rector of the oratory. "Often, thanks to him, they found new courage and managed to carry on when times were more difficult. To be lucky enough to visit with someone in whom we trust, someone in whom we can confide and be assured of being granted the support we need, is it not wonderful, to reach such blissful moments, exceptional instants of grace?"[17]

When the oratory celebrated both its hundredth anniversary and its dedication as a basilica in 2004, the archbishop of Montréal, Cardinal Jean-Claude Turcotte, spoke of the reason people had come to the oratory since the beginning. They were also the reasons people came to see Brother André when he was alive.

"People come here in search of God, in order to meet with Him," the cardinal said. "They come to entrust their sorrows, suffering, concerns, deceptions, illnesses, and weaknesses to Him. They come to pray for loved ones. They also come to thank Him for what they received from Him. They come for a word of comfort, a little light, or an act of pardon to enable them to continue on their path."[18]

What comes through these words, so expressive of the history of the oratory, is *mercy.* God's mercy is present and available there. His concern can be felt through the fatherly care of Saint Joseph and Brother André.

PART FOUR
HOLY LIVES

CHAPTER TEN

Rapt in Prayer

Pray without ceasing.

—1 Thessalonians 5:17

The works of the doorkeepers were ministries of prayer. They prayed for people and invited others to pray. Through these conduits of prayer flowed healing, reconciliation, comfort and hope. It's not surprising, then, that the doorkeepers led lives of intense and even mystical prayer.

For many years Brother André was sacristan of the community, a job in which he served several Masses a day, provided fresh flowers for the altar and cleaned the sacristy. He also rang the Angelus bells every day. When participating in liturgical prayer, André radiated joy. Someone once told Brother André that a light appeared around him when he prayed the stations of the cross.

And he spent long hours in prayer: after receiving Communion, before visiting the sick, before the Blessed Sacrament. He would kneel motionless and appear to focus completely on God. When riding in cars he would invite those with him to pray a rosary.

André recommended different devotions to different people, usually ones they were unused to. For himself, besides his bedrock devotions to Saint Joseph and the passion of Christ, he prayed to Mary, the Sacred Heart of Jesus and the Holy Spirit.

For his part Solanus practiced and recommended a wide range of devotions: the stations of the cross and prayers to the Sacred Heart, the Blessed Virgin Mary, Saint Ignatius Loyola, Saint Joseph, Saint Anthony of Padua, the Capuchin saints and the Little Flower, Saint Thérèse of the Child Jesus (of Lisieux). When Solanus spoke of God, Mary and Saint Joseph, it sounded as if he were talking about friends and family. In his prayer he drew all his troubled visitors into that family of faith and trust.

Solanus's prayer started early in the day, even by monastic standards. Frequently up and praying in the chapel before the rest of the community rose at 4:45 AM, he returned in the evening to pray for those he had met that day.

Very few of those who drove Solanus on visits to the sick or friends, or on trips to the countryside to gather supplies for the soup kitchen, could elude what Brother Leo Wollenweber called "holy travel." Like Brother André, Solanus prayed as he traveled, usually the rosary, and invited all those in the car to join him. Or he directed the driver to stop at a church so they could pray. On one occasion Solanus was late getting to the car for a trip with some other friars; as punishment the superior said the group would *not* say a rosary in the car.

Father Benedict Groeschel, the well-known Franciscan priest and writer, was a novice at St. Bonaventure's during Solanus's time there. One hot night Father Benedict could not sleep. At about three in the morning, he went for a walk and stopped at the friars' chapel to pray. Sensing someone else in the chapel, he turned on the lights and saw Solanus kneeling in front of the altar with his arms extended.

"His eyes were partly opened and he was gazing in the most intense way at the tabernacle." Solanus made no sign that he was in any way aware of Benedict, who turned off the light and left Solanus to his prayer.[1]

On another occasion the novices at St. Bonaventure's tested Solanus by walking in front of his praying form on the way to their places. So absorbed was Solanus in prayer that he never batted an eye. Sometimes people would have to shake him to bring him out of prayer. Friars would find Solanus laid out on the chapel floor at night, what charismatic Christians call being "slain in the Spirit" or "resting in the Spirit."[2]

While Solanus was traveling to Milwaukee, he stayed overnight at the Chicago home of his niece and her husband, the Conleys. At about two o'clock in the morning, Mr. Conley woke up and saw a light on in the living room. Going to turn it off, he found Solanus kneeling before a prayer book, his arms stretched over his head. He left Solanus alone and went back to bed. Arising a little before 6:00 AM to take Solanus to the train station, Mr. Conley found him in the same position. This time Solanus saw him and said, "Oh, are you up?…I will be finished in a few minutes."[3]

Padre Pio called himself a monk who prays, reflecting the attitude of all the doorkeepers. In their closeness to God, healing power flowed through them. Just as Brother André sometimes shone with light when he was in prayer, some said that Padre Pio "glowed with a strange fluorescent light, and that heat radiated out of his habit."[4]

CHAPTER ELEVEN

Humility

I didn't do the miracle. I only prayed for you.
The Lord healed you....I'm not God, nor am
I Jesus Christ. I'm a priest like any other
priest, no more and perhaps even less.
I don't perform miracles.

—Padre Pio

In looking at the lives of the doorkeepers, we see the meaning of true humility: being forgetful of self and always thinking of others—God and neighbor—first. This other-centeredness showed itself in the door-keepers' attitudes toward money and possessions, obedience and their sense of their spiritual gifts.

Poverty

Brother André strictly interpreted his vow of poverty, which he thought prohibited him from keeping or spending any money. He put any donations he received in a bag without even looking at the amount. When the bag was full, he turned it over to the oratory's bursar.

"How strange!" a woman once remarked. "Whether you give Brother André five cents or five hundred dollars, it's all the same to him."[1]

On a return trip from the United States, André stopped at Joseph Pichette's house to exchange the cash in his pocket for a check. He hardly spent anything when he traveled—railroad conductors and tollgate operators who knew him let him pass through for free—and he gave away medals and rosaries only with permission. He believed that possessions could distract from one's commitment to God.

Brother André wore his black soutane "until it was shiny with age and literally coming apart."[2] His black overcoat literally turned red from wear before he accepted a new one, with extreme reluctance, from his friend Azarias Claude. Pichette said he used the same wooden cup for close to twenty years.

The room he occupied as porter had a small bed, a table and a few chairs. During the oratory's construction he lived in a room over the chapel, which only later had a stove and a cupboard for spices and a few linens. This room also had two small iron beds, one for Brother André and one for sick men who stayed with him. If two sick men spent the night, André slept on a mattress on the floor without pillows or blankets.

When Solanus received money and gifts from people, he turned the money over to his superior—unless he forgot to. Sometimes the money ended up stuffed in his desk or used as bookmarks. One day Father Blase received permission from the superior to go through Solanus's room, and he found $153. Solanus "never said anything," Blase Gitzen remarked, "but I got the impression that he wasn't very pleased....Not that he cared about the money. He never took care of it because he couldn't care less. But I lost his place in many a book."[3]

When money came up in a sermon he heard, Solanus warned the homilist, "Don't talk money so much."[4]

He also gave away things to those who needed them. An acquaintance said, "I believe he followed the dictum of St. Francis that if you have something that you have no use for, give it away." "Everything he had," another said, "he gave away."[5]

In his room "there was nothing to speak of," a priest reported. His cell had a small bed, a desk and his typewriter, which stood on an upended crate. "There was nothing on his desk except a book of spiritual reading" and a small, handwritten sign that said, "Blessed be God in all His designs." "I would say that most of us had other books or we had little personal mementos in our room. Father Solanus had none of that."[6]

Solanus wore the same habit all the time. When it became worn, he held it together with safety pins until he could get it stitched up. When he traveled, he wore black clerical clothes, most likely the same ones that he had when he entered the Capuchins.

"In Quiet and Peace"

Brother André "'did not talk much,' and when he did, it was only 'of God.'" Much of the time he listened and smiled. He hesitated to join in conversation with the priests and brothers, "insisting...that such a humble brother as he had nothing of consequence to add to the discourse of such learned spiritual men."[7]

In 1920 Brother André attended a general meeting of the Congregation of Holy Cross at the University of Notre Dame in South Bend, Indiana. By this time his reputation for sanctity was long established, and the leaders asked him to say a few words to the delegates, who had sat through a long day of addresses and conferences. With the audience anticipating the words of this holy man, Brother André stood in front of his brethren and said there had been a lot of talking, and it was time for bed.[8]

In public events, even those associated with the oratory, it was hard to find Brother André; he was unobtrusive, standing on the edges. "Brother André was present only by obedience and in a very discreet manner."[9] Another observer said, "He never even stopped to admire [the oratory], nor did he ever ask one of his guests to acknowledge its beauty. I never heard him say when he spoke of the Oratory: my labor, my work. Again, to my knowledge, Brother André betrayed not the slightest curiosity concerning the amount of alms or donations collected for its construction."[10]

He felt uncomfortable when crowds gathered during his travels away from the oratory, and he once avoided a welcome-home party by returning a different way. Like Padre Pio, André hated to be photographed or interviewed; in fact, he was so shy that he could barely speak in public.

Thank God...and Saint Joseph
While André, Solanus and Pio had an awareness of the gifts God had given them, they never took credit for those gifts. "Don't thank me," Brother André would say.

"It is St. Joseph you must thank. Go and say a prayer to him." He complained, "How stupid people are to think that Brother André makes miracles. The Good God makes the miracles, St. Joseph obtains them, and I am only the wire which transmits their blessings."[11]

He responded to one interviewer's question about the cures, "It is through Saint Joseph. I am nothing but his little dog."[12] When someone once said to him that he was "even better than Saint Joseph," André became so distraught that he had to leave the office and go to bed.[13]

Solanus too made it clear to people seeking healing that, though he would gladly pray for them, it was only God who could cure. And Padre Pio said,

> Listen. God made all things. His creation includes the stars and the humblest domestic utensil. I belong to the second category....
>
> Don't think I am using rhetoric or speaking out of false modesty. I realize to the full the greatness of the gifts that God has bestowed upon me. But that terrifies me, because I know only too well what miserable use I have made of them. If He had given them to the lowest scoundrel in the world, he would have employed them better.[14]

In these men, it seemed, the greater the gifts, the greater the humility. While God had made them intercessors in ways only a few people experience, their sense of their own lowliness was more acute than most. All three of them wondered if they had used their gifts well.

All three prayed too, to the end of their lives, for their *true conversion*—when in the eyes of those who knew them they were already living saints. Pio called himself the "greatest sinner on earth" and said, "I am not good. I do not know why this habit of St. Francis, which I wear so unworthily, does not jump off of me. The last criminal in the world is nothing compared to me. Compared to me, he is a gentleman. Pray for me, that I might become good."[15]

When he heard talk of making him a saint, Pio said, "Before they make me a saint, they'll have to put Lucifer on the main altar of St. Peter's," and, "If they make me a saint, anyone who comes to me seeking a favor will have to bring me first of all a crate of macaroni. For each crate of macaroni, I'll grant a favor!"[16] When he received praise for building the hospital, he said to people, "You've done it yourselves. You gave the money and that's what is making the building go up....Let us give the honor to God. It was the Lord who made use of this stupid Padre Pio, for his own ends."[17]

God's Little Ones
The humility of the doorkeepers also expressed itself in their littleness. Vivian Bessette, a relative of Brother André, recalled the holy man's visit to her family home when she was a child in the Brighton Park neighborhood of Chicago. She recalled his playing games with the children. Typical of him when he stayed in others' homes, he refused special treatment. His worst fear when he was a guest, it seemed, was to be even the slightest burden to his hosts. At the Bessette home he insisted on sleeping on the floor and eating only bread and milk.

A striking story of the humility of both André and Solanus comes from the time they met. In 1935 André made one of his trips to visit family and friends and raise money for the oratory. Some of Solanus's friends from Windsor, Ontario, brought Brother André over the Detroit River to meet Solanus.

It is not clear how much English André knew, and Solanus spoke no French, but they did share a common language. Ever the dutiful Holy Cross brother, André knelt down to receive Father Solanus's blessing. Solanus, in a move highly unusual for a priest of his day, knelt down and asked André for his blessing. Whatever these two holy people knew of one another, it is as if holiness recognized itself in the other, not only in the gifts that flowed through them but also in their humility.

CHAPTER TWELVE

Grace in Suffering

In the crosses of life that come to us, Jesus offers us
opportunities to help him redeem the world.
Let us profit by his generosity.

—Solanus Casey

John McCaffery spoke of Padre Pio as "a man, martyred all his life, yes, as no mere human being was ever martyred before; but generous, compassionate, understanding, humorous."[1]

All the doorkeepers suffered, that is sure. They invited the sufferings of others into their lives. They endured chronic physical problems. Padre Pio, of course, not only suffered from illnesses but also bore the extraordinary pains of Christ's wounds. Brother André had his weak digestion, and Solanus Casey dealt for many years with recurring erysipelas, an acute skin disease that causes inflammation and fever, and other ailments.

In the passion of Jesus the doorkeepers found a key to understanding suffering. "It is better to suffer," Brother André sometimes told visitors. "We must be strong in trials, we must endure everything for the love of God who suffered so much for us."[2] Because Christ suffered for us, we can endure suffering. But Christ's suffering also moves us to try to relieve the pain of others.

André had a special devotion to the passion of Jesus and frequently told people the Passion story, at length and with great emotion. These talks were legendary, and he reserved them for people with crises of faith or shortcomings in their Christian living. He sometimes gave these people an hour of his time, much more than the few minutes he devoted to others. During these talks he pulled out of a drawer a "visual aid": a statue of the bleeding Christ. "Rarely," wrote Holy Cross Father Bergeron of Holy Cross, "could a sinner resist the authority of the frail old man who, with tears in his eyes, talked about the Passion of the Lord."[3]

The Padre's Persecution

Padre Pio's personal suffering was not limited to his wounds but also extended to the periods, off and on over a span of decades, when church authorities investigated and at times sanctioned him. The worst period occurred from the early 1920s to the 1930s.

The church has always been cautious about miracles, private revelations and the like, and there are plenty of examples of those who claimed such gifts and convinced others of them, only to be revealed later as delusional, fraudulent or worse. So in a sense it is understandable how some skepticism might have arisen when an obscure monk living in a remote town appeared as a stigmatist and wonder-worker of the first order.

The investigations of Padre Pio involved visitations from church officials, some at the behest of Pope Benedict XV, and even several medical examinations. When asked by his superiors, he duly submitted to what often became lengthy interrogations. Almost all those who interviewed him gave a favorable report.

One of his most ardent doubters was Franciscan Father Agostino Gemelli, founder of the Catholic University of Milan, a physician (the Gemelli hospital in Rome is named after him), psychologist and friend of Pope Pius IX. Gemelli judged Padre Pio to be a hysteric.

When Gemelli showed up at San Giovanni and insisted on seeing the padre's wounds, Pio, by now used to the protocols of examinations, insisted that he obtain proper written authorization. Thus rebuffed, Gemelli returned to Rome and wrote a report confirming his own prejudices and supporting Padre Pio's sanctions.

Another doctor, Amico Bignami, the University of Rome's chief pathologist, said Pio's stigmata were the result of autosuggestion. And the archbishop of Manfredonia, Pasquale Gagliardi, swore on his bishop's cross that Padre Pio had inflicted the wounds on himself and that the archbishop had seen the padre perfume himself (a most un-Capuchin act), thus explaining Pio's reputation for at times exuding an otherworldly scent. Some called Pio "a swindler, a hoax, a neurotic, and a victim of obsession."[4]

Pope Pius XI succeeded Pope Benedict in 1922, and shortly thereafter the Vatican's Holy Office passed an order to the Capuchin superior general that was a kind of ecclesiastical "death sentence" for Padre Pio. He could celebrate Mass only at irregular times and in private. He could not give public blessings or show, speak of or let people kiss his stigmata. He was to isolate himself in the monastery and break off all contact with his spiritual director, Father Benedetto, whom he never saw again on earth. Furthermore, his superiors were to move him to a monastery of significant distance from San Giovanni.

The Holy Office issued another decree, saying it could not "confirm…any basis for the supernatural character" of the phenomena surrounding Padre Pio and exhorting "the faithful to conform their practices to this declaration." This statement not only distanced the official church from Padre Pio but also humiliated the whole Capuchin order in Italy.[5]

House Arrest

The Capuchins decided to move Pio to a monastery at Ancona. When they sent the strapping Padre Luigi to San Giovanni to convey the order of the transfer, Pio said, even though it was midnight, "I'm at your disposal. Let's depart at once. When I am with my superior, I am with God."

When the shocked Padre Luigi asked where they would go in the middle of the night, Pio added, "I don't know. But I'll go with you, when and where you wish." Later he would write to Padre Luigi, "I don't think it is necessary for me to tell you how ready I am, thanks be to God, to obey whatever my superiors order me to do. For me, their voice is God's voice. I want to serve him faithfully until I die. With his help, I will obey whatever command I am given, even if it adds to all my suffering."[6]

But the Capuchins began having reservations about moving the padre, partly, it seems, because they feared the reaction of the citizens of San Giovanni, who clearly would use any means, even violent resistance, to keep Padre Pio in the town. In addition, the Capuchin superior at Ancona remarked somewhat wryly, "Ancona is not a place suitable for saints."[7]

In August the Holy Office suspended indefinitely the order to move Pio. Yet the office put out another condemnation in July 1924 and two years later condemned a book that had been written in defense of him.

The restrictions on Padre Pio lasted until 1937, and they struck at the heart of his ministry. He could not hear confessions, say Mass in public or talk to or exchange letters with any of the public. Over these long years several of Pio's friends, most of them laypeople, campaigned for his official rehabilitation.

Although Pio was essentially a prisoner in solitary confinement at the monastery, he did not listen to any criticism of the Vatican's treatment of him. To one of his supporters who spoke against church officials he said, "You did a wicked thing! We must respect the decrees of the Church. We must be silent and suffer!" To another: "Do all within the Church, act only within the Church! We must beware of putting ourselves against our Mother....Sweet is the hand of the Church, even when it batters us!"[8]

During the years of these restrictions, Padre Pio fulfilled his duties within the monastery and lived what for most Capuchins was a normal monastic life, though for Pio it was a kind of house arrest. Then two new books appeared, one detailing the church's opposition to Padre Pio. This book, not published in Italy, presented hundreds of letters to Rome from Catholics angry over the treatment of the padre. The other book, by a Dr. Festa, showed that Padre Pio's wounds eluded every natural cause that could be tested and concluded that they must be of supernatural origin.[9]

In addition, a Capuchin bishop gave Pope Pius XI a collection of affidavits from Pio's brother monks about his saintly life.

Finally the Vatican allowed Padre Pio to resume his ministerial life, a process that unfolded over several months. First he resumed celebrating Mass in public, then hearing confessions—of men, then of women. But suspicion pervaded even this resumption of his full priestly activities. No celebration with his friends was permitted; neither did he celebrate publicly his silver anniversary of ordination.

As Padre Pio reached his sixty-fifth birthday, in 1952, when one might expect that he could look back on a life of service to suffering souls, new problems were brewing for him. Resentment over the success of the *Casa*, along with a banking scandal in which the Capuchins had become unwittingly involved, led to charges that the padre and lay helpers were mismanaging hospital funds. A few years later others made charges about Pio's sexual morality and the nature of his relationship with some of his followers.

An investigation resulted in renewed sanctions on Padre Pio: no presiding at baptisms or weddings; no hearing the confessions of certain individuals; no Masses over half an hour long and no individual confessions over three minutes; no open contact with his followers. He also had to sign away title to the hospital.

Church authorities moved some monks friendly to Padre Pio to other monasteries, and Our Lady of Grace itself came under direct Vatican control. Again, only after a long and difficult campaign on the part of people loyal to the padre did the church lift the restrictions on him. This was in 1964, only four years before his death.

Fanatics, Not Friends

One other form of "persecution" visited upon Padre Pio was what the townspeople called *La Pie Donne,* the "holy women." These were women who literally fought their way to the front pews at Padre Pio's morning Mass, chained chairs to the Communion rail to secure a spot and hounded Pio on every occasion, clutching at him to get some part of his clothing or even his hair as a personal relic. They took up his time in the confessional and elsewhere talking of petty concerns.

Pio told these women on many occasions to go away. He literally had to fight them off, saying to them, "This is paganism! This is fanaticism!" He explained his reaction: "If we do not behave so, the people will eat us.... They squeeze my hand in a vise, they pull my arms, they press me on every side. I feel lost. I am forced to be rude. I'm sorry, but if I don't act this way, they'll kill me." "There should be a big fence around this area," he said, "with the sign, 'Lunatic Asylum.'"[10]

John McCaffery also called the *Pie Donne* fanatics. "They were emotional, superstitious, and prime examples of that category of person who hurt and angered

Padre Pio *by stopping at him,* as it were, *instead of using him as a steppingstone to God.*"[11]

In 1960, just before Padre Pio's fiftieth anniversary of ordination, the *Pie Donne* were becoming increasingly unruly and creating scandal and embarrassment for the church. Padre Agostino, the minister provincial, was using more and more violent language when he stood in the choir loft and shouted down at the pious ladies to keep them in line. The scuffling for position at the padre's appearances caused an injury to the wife of the Chilean ambassador, who later told Padre Pio: "Now I know why you built the hospital across the street."[12]

Apparently some of the pious ladies were also jealous that Cleonice Morcaldi, the mayor's wife, and two of her friends were monopolizing opportunities to talk with Padre Pio. In retaliation they started a rumor about a sexual relationship between the padre and Cleonice.

These happenings prompted the Vatican to order yet another investigation. The Holy See sent Monsignor Carlo Maccari to look into the matter of the "holy women" and another matter of concern, the financial management of the hospital. The situation was complicated, but the subjects of the accusations had not changed much: Pio's relations with his followers and money.

Brother André had his own version of *La Pie Donne* to deal with. These were some of the Little Sisters of the Holy Family, who performed services for the college community. They cut pieces off the clothing he sent for cleaning and saved his hair and nail clippings, which they gave away as "relics." André called these sisters "thieves." He asked one of the priests, "Tell me, what can they do with my hair? I don't even have enough to make a pillow!"[13]

These holy men inspired intense devotion, but the line between healthy and unhealthy enthusiasm for a person is clear. Their witness always pointed to Christ, not to themselves. They knew where their immense gifts came from and to what purpose they possessed them: to bring others to God. Stop with Padre Pio or Brother André or Father Solanus, and you miss God.

More representative of the devoted followers of Padre Pio were those who quietly attached themselves to him and cooperated with him in all the good works emanating from San Giovanni: the hospital, training schools for young people, the choirs, concerts and plays. André and Solanus too had their devoted helpers, also usually laypeople, who worked in soup kitchens, helped build a place of prayer, raised money and drove them to sick calls, among other activities.

Consider It Joy

Another kind of harassment Padre Pio endured in his later years had to do with his caretakers. Like any aging friar, he needed the help of another friar. Padre Eusebio was his first infirmarian. Eusebio had a deep veneration for Padre Pio, and Pio loved him dearly.

After some years of this arrangement, however, a new Capuchin minister general, an American, took office and began a campaign to straighten out what he saw as a number of problems in the Italian Capuchin communities. One Sicilian community had engaged in smuggling, and several Capuchin houses had lost money through investments with a fraudulent financier.

The general also thought the Monastery of Our Lady of Grace, with Padre Pio at its center, needed reform, so he interrogated the friars, insisted on the strict following of friary rules and instructed some friars to report to him directly.

The worst part for Padre Pio was the transfer of his beloved Padre Eusebio to another community on the odd grounds that Eusebio was interposing himself between Padre Pio and those who came to visit him. Padre Pio was devastated; he became sick and depressed. "Tell them," Padre Pio said to his friend John McCaffery, when the latter was going to the Vatican to intercede for the restoration of Padre Eusebio, "that if they want to put me in the tomb, this is the shortest road."[14]

Padre Eusebio's replacement as caregiver was Padre Pellegrino. He was truly devoted to his tasks as a friar and as the caretaker of Padre Pio. Yet while Eusebio was emotional and outgoing, willing to poke gentle fun at Padre Pio and got him to take care of himself, Pellegrino was serious and reserved.

André and Solanus also endured more serious misunderstanding within their communities. Recall the ridicule André endured for his use of blessed oil.

Some of Solanus's brother friars did not enjoy his violin playing during their recreation periods, and they turned up the radio to give Solanus the message. Some made fun of him for putting all his food in one bowl or for being late for meals, even when he had been helping someone in need. In his last years in Detroit, words bordered on the cruel, despite the fact that Solanus was by this time well-known for his sanctity.

Whether their own or others, the afflictions the door-keepers suffered did not discourage them. Despite what was going on in and around them, they showed great strength and devotion to their tasks and an unwavering concern for the legions of people who sought succor from them. Moreover, all were joyful people.

"Brother André seemed…in a state of incomparable joy."[15] André himself said, "Never give way to sadness. Always be cheerful and avoid giving pain to anyone."[16]

When friars criticized Solanus for playing the violin, he went to the chapel and played by himself before the Blessed Sacrament. When a head porter called him an "old fraud" and told him that no one could understand him because of his weak voice, Solanus replied, "God understands me."[17]

These holy men felt emotions, their own and others', very deeply. Almost all of their time with visitors was taken up with hearing about illness, death, troubles, sins and the like. Contrasting strongly with this daily environment was their joy and serenity. They could say with Saint James, "Whenever you face trials of any kind, consider it nothing but joy, because you know that the testing of your faith produces endurance; and let endurance have its full effect, so that you may be mature and complete, lacking in nothing" (James 1:2–4).

CHAPTER THIRTEEN

Holy Deaths

My work is done. And besides, if you can do
things here, just think of how much
you can do in heaven.

—Brother André

As the 1930s began and Brother André entered into his late eighties, his fragile health began to deteriorate even further. He frequently suffered from angina, headaches, nausea, dizziness and fainting spells. André resisted medication and doctor's commands, as he had his whole life, though he was in constant heart and stomach pain. During this period he also had bouts of gastritis and double pneumonia, and his poor diet caused stomach and liver disorders. He developed a raspy voice, which made him difficult to understand.

In the last few years of his life, chronic illness and failing hearing could cause him to lose his temper, though sometimes the people who visited him were the provocation. "Do you think that I'm God?" he once said to someone demanding healing. "*I* don't perform miracles. I only pray."[1] To another person he said, "I'm going to pray to the Good God to grant you the gift of intelligence."[2]

Like Padre Pio, André had little time for those who came out of curiosity, were abusive or obnoxious or wouldn't stop talking. Near the end of his days a nurse told him she would never have been able to see as many people as he did. André admitted, "Sometimes it's very hard. If only people came straight to the point. But they insist on giving their names, saying where they come from, adding that they took the train....Unfortunately, there's such misery!"[3]

After one display of irritation on André's part, a woman exclaimed, "But he *can't* be angry. He's a saint." Brother André recognized this weakness in himself. He said to a reporter: "Impatience is my great besetting sin."[4] At the end of the day he sometimes wept in his room because "I made somebody cry today." He would ask a priest if he could still receive Communion after getting angry with a visitor.[5]

Faithful to the End

The beginning of the end came in the summer of 1935. Brother André fainted while eating dinner at the home of a cousin—who had been healed years earlier through André's intercession—near Montréal. Though André eventually returned to work at the oratory, he stopped keeping regular office hours and saw visitors or made sick calls only on occasion.

With the approval of his superior, he spent a lot of time at the home of his friends, the Pichettes. Despite his age and condition, some members of the Holy Cross community thought this arrangement improper for a vowed religious. Like Solanus, age, physical decline and a lifetime of service did not protect him from the criticisms of some of his colleagues.

Brother André did get some relief when a new superior, the young Father Albert Cousineau, asked him to keep office hours at the oratory two days a week. André, who "had felt ignored and irrelevant and had appeared especially depressed and grumpy," returned to living all the time at the rectory and "now seemed his old self."[6]

At this time a severe shortfall of funds struck the oratory. Father Cousineau responded by putting to work his considerable organizational and business skills, and Brother André mobilized his own techniques. A group prayed the rosary and processed with the statue of Saint Joseph on Mount Royal, and André suggested putting a statue of the saint in the midst of the unfinished basilica. The harsh Canadian winter was approaching, and André reasoned, "Once he is placed there in the cold and snow, if Saint Joseph wants to be covered, he will see to it."[7]

André advised Father Cousineau to hold a medal of Joseph in his hand when he visited the archbishop to request a loan. The archbishop granted the loan.

On January 1, 1937, it was clear that Brother André was nearing death. He had sensed the end was coming. On his last trip to the United States, he had said while handing out Saint Joseph medals, "These are the last medals I'm ever going to give."[8]

His Holy Cross superiors decided he could not receive proper care at the oratory, so they moved him to the hospital of St-Laurent, operated by the Sisters of Good Hope. André had passed this place some days earlier on a hospital call. "What a beautiful place to go to die," he had said of the small, houselike building.[9]

Wrapped from head to toe in blankets during his transport to the hospital, he said, "I look like someone going to the North Pole."[10] Two days later, in his hospital bed, he said, "The Great Almighty is coming!"[11]

Even at the end he remained clearheaded with visitors, compassionate and humble. He retained his sense of humor: "It's your old nuisance calling you again," he said to a nurse who had responded to his call.[12]

After his first and only dose of morphine, he told the doctors, "Do not give me drugs," and, "I have more faith in prayer than in pills." His condition was such, however, that no remedy helped him. "I can do nothing," he replied to a nurse who asked why he didn't go to Saint Joseph to heal him. He was living out the counsel he had given to many sufferers over the years: "Sickness is a good thing, because it helps us to reflect on our past life and make reparations through penitence and through suffering."[13]

To those who visited him, including his superior, he made an extraordinary request: "Pray for my conversion."[14] One is reminded of Padre Pio, who at the end of his life asked his friend Pietro Cugino, "Tell me seriously, do you think I'll be saved?"[15] Or of Solanus, who, when he made his annual retreat in 1945, after his transfer from Detroit to Brooklyn, said he might "try again to be converted for another year."[16]

Final Good-byes

On the morning of January 5, Brother André became unconscious, and Father Charron conferred last rites.

At this point the hospital allowed the public to visit the dying man, and perhaps up to a thousand people, certainly hundreds, walked through his room, some of whom touched his hands and feet with religious articles and asked him, "Good Brother André, when you're in heaven, remember me!"[17]

In the company of his old friend Joseph Pichette; some of his Holy Cross confreres, including Father Adolphe Clément, who were praying the Litany of the Dead; three doctors and two hospital sisters, Brother André died at 12:50 AM on January 6, 1937, the Solemnity of the Epiphany. His last words were "Oh Mary! My sweet Mother and Mother of my Savior, have mercy on me; save me" and a prayer to Saint Joseph.[18] At the moment of death Joseph Pichette touched Brother André's lips with the crucifix he had been holding.

After his death thousands of people, some of whom had been keeping vigil outside the hospital, walked past his body in a repeat of the day before. Out of respect for this person who had stayed so close to suffering and illness and who had brought consolation to those facing chronic sickness, disfigurement, even death, the community decided not to embalm his body.

The casket stood in the crypt near the entrance of the oratory, and a million people came to view his body. Sick people came to pray, conversions took place and people left intentions on pieces of paper or touched his body with rosaries and medals. Hundreds left crutches, canes and other tokens of the healings they had experienced.

It was an unprecedented event in the history of French

Canada. Cardinal Villeneuve, the archbishop of Québec, could not get close to the coffin. He said to Father Cousineau, "I have often read in the lives of the saints that so great a concourse of people came to view their remains that the high prelates could not get near them. I always thought it was a pious exaggeration, but yesterday evening it was proved to me to be authentic."[19]

At the Requiem Mass celebrated in the oratory, the assembly included the mayor of Montréal, the Canadian secretary of state and Maurice Duplessis, Québec's prime minister and a former Notre-Dame-des-Neiges student. In his homily Cardinal Villeneuve said,

> We may say that today we celebrate the feast of humility.
>
> On the tomb which guards the mortal remains of this virtuous Apostle of Saint Joseph, Brother André, we may read these words: "*Pauper, Servus, Humilis*". *Pauper,* that is to say, "poor," the religious that we so often came to see at the Oratory; *Servus,* "servant," the…brother, the last in rank in his community; *Humilis,* so little in his own eyes, without any suspicion of the throngs his death would bring together.…
>
> No prince of the Church or of the State could have a funeral such as this.…Remember then Brother André's words and hear him repeating them to us still:…Go to Joseph.[20]

The first location of Brother André's tomb was in the oratory's crypt, under artist Henri Charlier's mural of the death of Saint Joseph. When the cause for André's beatification opened, however, the location of the tomb became a question. The church discourages open veneration of those considered for beatification, so as not to seem to be anticipating the results or unduly influencing the official decision. To address this situation the oratory began construction of a votive chapel in 1945.

Votive comes from the Latin word *votum*, meaning "vow," and refers to anything expressing a vow, wish or prayer. The oratory's votive chapel, completed in 1950, houses much of what represents the prayers, promises and expressions of thanksgiving of those touched by the healing ministry of the oratory and its founder: Brother André's relocated tomb along with hundreds of discarded canes and crutches, as well as banks of candles.

Joseph Pichette summed up Brother André's earthly life in this way: "The daily repetition of all his acts of charity towards his neighbour, the way he received visitors throughout the day, his hearing nothing but complaints and the long evening prayers at the Oratory, all show his heroism in the practice of charity."[21]

Pope John Paul II beatified Brother André on May 23, 1982, before thirty thousand pilgrims in St. Peter's Square. The next month fifty thousand people assembled in Montréal's Olympic Stadium to honor Blessed André, some of whom had known him personally.

Death Can Be Beautiful

Throughout his life, but especially, as one would expect, toward the end, Solanus Casey's thoughts turned more and more to death and to how life relates to death. His statements on this subject show a remarkable familiarity, even friendliness, with death, which well reflect the words of his spiritual father Saint Francis of Assisi, who prayed in his *Canticle of Brother Sun*, "Be praised, my

Lord, for our Sister Bodily Death, from whom no one living can escape."[22]

"Many are the rainbows," Solanus wrote in a letter to his brother Edward, "the sunbursts, the gentle breezes—and the hailstorms we are liable to meet before, by the grace of God, we shall be able to tumble into our graves with the confidence of tired children into their places of peaceful slumber."[23]

While still in Yonkers he had written, "Death can be beautiful...if we make it so." How? A passage from another letter answers this question: "Let us thank God ahead of time for whatever He foresees is pleasing to Him,...leaving everything at His divine disposal, including—with all its circumstances, when, where, and how—God may be pleased to dispose the events of our death."[24]

At the beginning of 1956, Solanus's skin disease worsened to the point that his superiors in Huntington felt he should go back to Detroit. On January 12 he left St. Felix's in the company of a Capuchin brother. In Detroit he underwent an operation to deal with some cancerous lesions on his legs, but as for the rest of the problems, the doctors said they could do little beyond trying to keep him comfortable. Far fewer antibiotics were available then, and Solanus was allergic to the ones that were.

In order to protect Solanus, the superior forbade the community, Solanus included, from saying anything about his presence at St. Bonaventure's. He could not meet with people or receive phone calls without permission, though he did start to answer some of his correspondence.

It soon proved impossible to completely conceal Solanus's presence at the monastery. People started calling and ringing the doorbell, asking to see him. When Solanus was up to it, his superior allowed half-hour talks or visits to his room. Solanus chafed a bit at the restrictions on what had been his calling. "Why don't they let me see the people?" he asked Brother Ignatius Milne, who sensed in Solanus's tone the idea, "So what if I die in the process? What am I all about?"[25]

The lid on the secret return of Solanus came off in a big way in December 1956. The *Detroit News* was doing a story on the hundredth anniversary of the Capuchin foundation in the United States and sent a photographer to take some pictures at St. Bonaventure's. The photographer spotted the picturesque Solanus, though he apparently didn't know who Solanus was. He asked Solanus to pose as if he were giving a blessing.

Solanus stiffened a bit and said, "I will not *pretend* to give a blessing. If you want a blessing, kneel down and I will give one." The photographer shot his photo of "Father Solanus giving a real blessing."

The monastery chronicle a few days later told the story: "The Capuchins of Detroit 'made the papers' today. Father Solanus was spread all over the front cover of the [color] section." Solanus was also the only friar quoted in the article, saying Capuchin life was "like starting heaven here on earth."[26] The Capuchin brothers at the front desk now had to fend off larger numbers of people trying to see Solanus.

"My Last Breath to God"

In early May 1957 Solanus suffered a severe outbreak of erysipelas, and he entered the hospital, where his condition became grave. After receiving oxygen, he improved a bit, and as he came to he began singing a hymn to Mary. He was even able to joke with people. To a nursing sister who said, "Father, throughout the years I have so often heard people speak of you," he replied, perhaps recalling his prison-guard days, "Yes, people often speak of Jesse James, too." Another time this same sister came to his room and asked, "How about a blessing?" "All right," Solanus said, "I'll take one."[27]

He was in and out of the hospital a couple more times, and even there his ministry continued. Patients came to him for prayers and blessings, some of which resulted in favors granted. He liked to be wheeled to the hospital chapel, and he would bless people along the way. In the chapel he attended Mass, prayed the rosary or had someone read to him from *Mystical City of God*. His life was much like what it had been for decades: prayer, holy reading and blessing people who sought him out.

Solanus was in a great deal of pain near his death, but he never complained. He maintained his spirituality of gratitude to the end. When asked where it hurt, he said, "My whole body hurts," and added, "Thanks be to God."[28]

Like many people near death, Solanus seemed to know when the end was coming. On the day before he died, he told his friend and superior Gerald Walker, "Tomorrow will be a beautiful day."[29] He also said, "Tomorrow it will be all over. I want to go to heaven, but with all Christendom."[30] What did he mean? "I am offering my sufferings that all might be one. Oh, if only I could live to see the conversion of the whole world."[31]

As he had throughout his whole life and ministry, Solanus was offering himself in order to bring others to God. His words to Gerald Walker sum up his life: "I looked on my whole life as giving, and I want to give until there is nothing left of me to give. So I prayed that, when I come to die, I might be perfectly conscious, so that with a deliberate act I can give my last breath to God."[32]

God answered his prayer, for at the moment of his death, on July 31, 1957, Solanus suddenly opened his eyes, reached out his arms and said: "I give my soul to Jesus Christ."[33] He died fifty-three years to the hour after his first Mass as a priest in Appleton, Wisconsin. The perfect self-offering of his earthly life was complete.

As Solanus's body was being prepared, it was discovered that his skin disease had disappeared. Solanus was waked first at a funeral home, where people began lining up at five o'clock in the morning on the day of the visitation, and then at St. Bonaventure Chapel, where about twenty thousand people viewed the body.

All kinds of people came: "ordinary people, rich people, women, children, priests; every class of people. There was nothing done directly or indirectly by any member of the [Capuchin] Community to encourage such a gathering. This was an entirely spontaneous outpouring of love and respect by the people who came to see him."[34] The celebration of the funeral Mass took place amid an overflow crowd on the following Saturday.

The public outpouring of grief and gratitude genuinely surprised some of the friars. They had not realized how many people Solanus had touched and what a profoundly holy and venerable figure they had had in their midst. In contrast to Padre Pio, whom virtually the entire monastic community at Our Lady of Grace revered, Solanus from time to time had received the treatment due a second-class citizen.

Within a year after Solanus's death, Father Gerald Walker sent a report to the Capuchin minister general in Rome, Father Benignus of Sant' Ilario. In a return letter Father Benignus wrote,

> Solanus was certainly an extraordinary man, a replica of St. Francis, a real Capuchin. The wonderful spontaneous tribute paid to him by Catholic and non-Catholic alike is surely an ample proof that our traditional spirituality is still very much capable of winning the people among whom we work to a realization of the primacy of the spiritual and Catholic outlook on life. May he still continue to do much good from heaven, bringing many souls nearer to God and inspiring his own Capuchin brothers with something of his humble spirit.[35]

A "Peaceful and Sweet" Departure

On many days throughout his life, especially as he aged, Padre Pio appeared ill and weak. Sometimes those who had not seen him for a while were convinced that they would not see him alive again. "So many times he would be low," one friar said, "and then the Lord would spruce him up…, so we had no indication that death was near."[36]

It was with shock, then, that on the night of September 22, 1968, those around Padre Pio realized he was dying. By the beginning of that month, he had stopped eating, being unable to keep much food down—the same problem he had suffered as a young man. His asthma attacks caused chest pain, rapid heartbeat, cold sweats and difficulty breathing.

Still, his physician, Dr. Sala, said he did not see why the padre should be dying then more than at any other time the doctor had known him. He had celebrated Mass on the previous day, a day that had seen a large gathering of Padre Pio prayer groups at San Giovanni.

Padre Pellegrino was sitting with Padre Pio when he asked to make his confession. He then said once again the words of his religious profession, asked Padre Pellegrino to ask for the forgiveness of any members of his community he might have hurt and conveyed his blessing to all his spiritual sons and daughters. Though it was only a little after midnight, he asked Pellegrino if he had said Mass yet. "This morning you will say Mass for me," he said.[37]

Although severe arthritis had more or less confined Pio to a wheelchair, he rose from bed and put on his habit without help, said he wanted to go for a walk on the terrace, walked across the hallway and turned on the light for the terrace. The two priests sat on the terrace for a few minutes, then Padre Pio suddenly became weak again.

Pellegrino had a challenge getting him back to his cell. There Pio's breathing became more difficult. Over Pio's objections, Padre Pellegrino went to get the superior and another friar. He also called Dr. Sala.

As Padre Pio was failing, he began saying quietly the names of Jesus and Mary over and over again. When Pellegrino returned to the cell and saw what was happening, he called the hospital. Two more doctors came to assist, but their efforts were in vain.

The whole community of friars came to Padre Pio's cell, knelt around him and prayed. With a rosary in his hands and the holy names of Jesus and Mary on his lips, Padre Pio experienced a death that one of the doctors called "the most peaceful and sweet I have ever seen."[38]

After Padre Pio died, his wounds disappeared. According to Father Pellegrino, "When Dr. Sala and I were preparing his body after he died, a last scale fell from his hand. We checked his feet, his hands, and his side very carefully. The skin looked as new as a baby's skin. You couldn't see anything where the wounds had been, not even the slightest trace of a scar."[39]

Actually, the visible wounds had started healing about a year before Pio's death, though the pain remained. Scabs had been falling from his hands during his last Mass. Padre Onorato, one of Pio's helpers, commented, "The ministry was finished, so the signs were finished."[40]

Four days later Padre Pio was buried in the crypt underneath the main altar of the monastery church. Today San Giovanni Rotondo is the second most visited shrine in Roman Catholicism, surpassed only by the Basilica of Our Lady of Guadalupe in Mexico City. As in life, Padre Pio continues to draw millions who seek his help or wish to express thanks for his intercession.

Our Brothers in Christ

It was as much the *humanity* of the doorkeepers as it was their supernatural gifts that attracted people to them. The human beings André, Solanus and Pio showed people God and inspired them to lead lives of holiness.

One of Padre Pio's former students from his early days as a teacher, Father Aurelio Di Ioria, said, "He cast a spell over people. There was just something about him—a charm, a spell. It was only later that people considered him a saint. We boys were attracted to him in those days because he was very human, because he could understand us. He was very good with everybody. The key to his charm was his humanity. His sanctity was his humanity."[41]

Similarly, one of his biographers, Bernard Ruffin, wrote, "Those who knew Padre Pio well, loved him not because of his mystical gifts but because he was a wise, good, unassuming, and amiable Christian gentleman, who, through his virtues (as much or more than by supernatural phenomena) led men and women closer to God."[42]

To see the doorkeepers only as wonder-workers and healers is to miss the totality of who they were and what their lives mean today. Certainly the healings were the immediate reason poor, afflicted and troubled people who had nowhere else to turn came to them in such numbers. Though the miracles took center stage, what went on behind the scenes was just as important.

An American inner-city teacher wrote:

When we think of Blessed André, we naturally consider his role as a healer. As well we should. But, because of my profession, I am more interested in the doorkeeper, the school handyman. The little guy who says his rosary while he maintains the school's grounds. The fellow who cuts the kids' hair, and speaks to them of Saint Joseph. The brother who takes a student for a walk up the slope of Mount Royal, and with this kid says *The Little Office of Mary*. Forty years he spent doing this.[43]

The doorkeepers demonstrated what can happen when people are full of God. Through their ministry people came closer to God, especially through prayer, and felt empowered to respond to the presence of God in their hearts and minds by living out their faith. Padre Pio's long hours hearing confessions stand as a symbol of what all the doorkeepers brought people: *reconciliation*—not only forgiveness of their sins but *acceptance* of their situations.

This, then, is the first gift the doorkeepers offer us: the power of faith to heal not only spectacularly but also in the form of acceptance, trust in God, gratitude and joy even in the midst of suffering. Give thanks ahead of time. Blessed be God in all his designs. Go to Joseph; he will never leave you out in the cold. Thank God always, no matter what happens.

The doorkeepers showed how *humility* means a total openness to God and others. They gave themselves completely in prayer and patient service, all the time, day after day, decade after decade. And thus their second lesson: the blessedness of other-centeredness, of living for others and being available for others, even when doing so is extremely difficult. This self-offering is at the heart of Christian living.

Their humility also expressed itself in their utter simplicity. When we have God, they say to us, we really do not need much else—materially, emotionally or in any other way. Padre Pio came from one of the poorest regions of Italy and spent most of his life at a small friary outside a remote village. He wore a habit that had changed little since the Middle Ages and followed a rule that Saint Francis had devised eight hundred years before. He hardly ever left the monastery, let alone the town (at least in his body!). Yet over the years millions of people came to him and continue to do so, seeking his traditional piety and wisdom.

Solanus Casey wore the same Capuchin habit and followed the same rule. He lived in the inner city and in small Midwestern towns. He spent most of his life sitting in an office talking to the sick and troubled people who came to him.

Brother André's superiors had barely let the under-educated laborer join the Holy Cross order. André devoted himself to serving his community and children. For years he stood behind a desk in an office, offering the afflicted prayer, care and counsel.

"All who humble themselves will be exalted" (Luke 18:14). We see this clearly in the lives of the doorkeepers. When André's sainthood cause went to Rome, for example, a mountain of recommendations went with it. Two cardinals, eight future cardinals, twelve archbishops, seventy-three bishops, the chief justice of the Canadian supreme court, the lieutenant governor of Québec, a former Québec prime minister and prominent political, cultural and educational figures were among those sending 245 letters urging the formal opening of his cause. Even Étienne Gilson, the great scholar of religion and member of the French Academy, sent a letter expressing his admiration for Brother André. The Vatican also received a petition on André's behalf bearing 578,861 names.[44]

André, Solanus and Pio came from marginal beginnings, and they struggled a bit to find their way. They faced failure and hostility. Yet they knew what they wanted to do: to dwell in the house of the Lord and serve God and God's people, especially the poor in body and spirit. Our true vocations can emerge in doing the same.

Appendix

What follows are three ecclesiastically approved prayers to André Bessette (feast day: January 6), Solanus Casey and Saint Pio of Pietrelcina (feast day: September 23), along with information on how to contact the organizations that are helping to preserve their legacies.

Father, you have chosen Brother André to spread devotion to Saint Joseph and to minister to all those who are afflicted. Through his intercession, grant us the favor we are now requesting. We also pray that the church may canonize him. Grant us the grace to imitate his piety and charity so that, with him, we may share the reward promised to all those who care for their neighbor because of their love for you.

Saint Joseph's Oratory of Mount Royal
3800, Queen Mary Road
Montréal, Québec H3V 1H6
Canada
www.saint-joseph.org

O God, I adore you. I give myself to you. May I be the person you want me to be, and may your will be done in my life today.

Thank you for the gifts you gave to Father Solanus. If it is your will, glorify him on earth so that others will carry on his love for the poor, lonely and suffering in our world. In order that others will joyfully accept your divine plan, I ask you to hear this prayer through Jesus Christ, Our Lord. Amen.

The Solanus Casey Center
1780 Mt. Elliott Street
Detroit, MI 48207-3496
www.solanuscasey.org

O God, you gave Saint Pio of Pietrelcina the grace of participating in a unique way in the passion of your Son. Through his intercession, may we conform ourselves to the death of Jesus, so that we may also share in the glory of the Resurrection. We ask this through Christ our Lord, who lives and reigns with you and the Holy Spirit, one God, forever and ever. Amen.

The National Centre for Padre Pio
111 Barto Road
Barto, PA 19504
www.padrepio.org

Friary of the Capuchin Friars Minor Santa Maria delle Grazie
San Giovanni Rotondo, Italy
www.conventopadrepio.com

Notes

Introduction

1. Quoted in Michael Crosby, ed., *Solanus Casey: The Official Account of a Virtuous American Life* (New York: Crossroad, 2000), p. 192.

2. Quoted in C. Bernard Ruffin, *Padre Pio: The True Story*, revised and expanded (Huntington, Ind.: Our Sunday Visitor, 1991), p. 196.

3. Quoted in Crosby, *Solanus Casey*, p. 253.

4. Quoted in Claire Vanier, "Brother André: Like a Fountain," *The Oratory*, vol. 77, no. 4 (July–August 2003), p. 9.

5. Quoted in C. Bernard Ruffin, *The Life of Brother André: The Miracle Worker of St. Joseph* (Huntington, Ind.: Our Sunday Visitor, 1988), p. 106.

6. John McCaffery, *Tales of Padre Pio: The Friar of San Giovanni* (Garden City, N.Y.: Image, 1981), p. 205.

7. McCaffery, p. 173.

8. Quoted in Crosby, *Solanus Casey*, p. 141.

9. Joseph Olivier Pichette, *Brother André as I Knew Him: Joseph Olivier Pichette's Testimony* (Montréal: St. Joseph's Oratory, 2003), p. 35.

10. Quoted in McCaffery, p. 118.

11. Clement I, quoting an unknown source, in "The Letter of the Church of Rome to the Church of Corinth," commonly called Clement's First Letter, 46, in Cyril Richardson, *Early Christian Fathers* (New York: Macmillan, 1975), p. 65.

Part One: BEGINNINGS

Chapter One: A Working Brother

1. Quoted in Jean-Guy Dubuc, *Brother André,* Robert Prud'homme, trans. (Montréal: Fides, 1999), p. 30.

2. Quoted in Ruffin, *Life of Brother André,* p. 14.

3. Quoted in Ruffin, *Life of Brother André,* p. 15.

4. Quoted in Ruffin, *Life of Brother André,* p. 16.

5. Quoted in Ruffin, *Life of Brother André,* p. 17.

6. Quoted in Ruffin, *Life of Brother André,* p. 21.

7. Quoted in Dubuc, p. 35.

8. Quoted in Ruffin, *Life of Brother André,* p. 17.

9. Dubuc, p. 35.

10. Quoted in Ruffin, *Life of Brother André,* p. 18.

11. Quoted in Ruffin, *Life of Brother André,* p. 22.

12. Quoted in Ruffin, *Life of Brother André,* p. 23.

13. Quoted in Ruffin, *Life of Brother André,* p. 23.

14. Quoted in Dubuc, p. 48.

15. Quoted in Dubuc, p. 49.

16. Quoted in Ruffin, *Life of Brother André,* p. 29.

17. Quoted in Ruffin, *Life of Brother André,* p. 29.

18. Quoted in Ruffin, *Life of Brother André,* p. 30.

19. Ruffin, *Life of Brother André,* p. 35.

20. Quoted in Ruffin, *Life of Brother André,* p. 36.

21. Quoted in Ruffin, *Life of Brother André,* p. 38.

22. Ruffin, *Life of Brother André,* p. 39.

23. Quoted in Ruffin, *Life of Brother André,* p. 37.

24. Ruffin, *Life of Brother André,* p. 129.

25. Quoted in Ruffin, *Life of Brother André,* p. 128.

26. Quoted in Ruffin, *Life of Brother André,* p. 129.

27. Vanier, p. 9.

Chapter Two: "Go to Detroit"

1.   Leo Wollenweber, *Meet Solanus Casey: Spiritual Counselor and Wonder Worker* (Cincinnati: Servant, 2002), p. 20.

2.   Quoted in Michael H. Crosby, *Thank God Ahead of Time: The Life and Spirituality of Solanus Casey* (Chicago: Franciscan Press, 1985), p. 6.

3.   Crosby, *Solanus Casey,* p. 25.

4.   Quoted in Crosby, *Solanus Casey,* p. 27.

5.   Quoted in Crosby, *Solanus Casey,* p. 38.

6.   Crosby, *Solanus Casey,* p. 37.

7.   Quoted in Crosby, *Solanus Casey,* p. 41.

8.   Quoted in Crosby, *Solanus Casey,* p. 43.

9.   Quoted in Wollenweber, p. 32.

10. Quoted in Wollenweber, p. 33.

11. Wollenweber, p. 33.

12. Letter of Father Benignus of Sant' Ilario following Father Solanus's death, quoted in Wollenweber, p. 113.

13. Quoted in Crosby, *Solanus Casey,* p. 46, emphasis added.

14. Quoted in Crosby, *Thank God,* p. 285.

15. Crosby, *Thank God,* p. 285.

16. Quoted in Crosby, *Thank God,* pp. 285–286.

17. Quoted in Crosby, *Solanus Casey,* p. 49.

18. Quoted in Crosby, *Solanus Casey,* p. 50.

19. Quoted in Crosby, *Solanus Casey,* pp. 49–50.

20. Quoted in Crosby, *Solanus Casey,* p. 51.

Chapter Three: Into the Mountains

1. Quoted in Ruffin, *Padre Pio,* p. 25.
2. Quoted in Renzo Allegri, *Padre Pio: A Man of Hope* (Cincinnati: Servant, 2000), p. 11.
3. Allegri, p. 13.
4. Quoted in Allegri, p. 21.
5. Quoted in Allegri, p. 24.
6. Duchess of St. Albans, *Magic of a Mystic: Stories of Padre Pio* (New York: Clarkson Potter, 1983), p. 35.
7. Quoted in St. Albans, p. 35.
8. Quoted in Ruffin, *Padre Pio,* pp. 51–52.
9. Quoted in Ruffin, *Padre Pio,* p. 55.
10. Quoted in Allegri, p. 54.
11. Quoted in Ruffin, *Padre Pio,* p. 103.
12. St. Albans, p. 38.
13. Ruffin, *Padre Pio,* p. 39.
14. Quoted in Allegri, p. 44.
15. Quoted in Allegri, p. 59.
16. St. Albans, p. 41.
17. Quoted in Allegri, p. 62.
18. Katharina Tangari, *Stories of Padre Pio,* John Collorafi, trans. (Rockford, Ill.: Tan, 1997), p. 18.

Part Two: EVERYDAY MIRACLES
Chapter Four: "Get Up and Walk"

1. Dubuc, p. 53.
2. Pichette, p. 43.
3. Ruffin, *Life of Brother André,* pp. 40–41.
4. Dubuc, p. 52.
5. Dubuc, p. 54.
6. Quoted in Ruffin, *Life of Brother André,* p. 42.

7.   Quoted in Ruffin, *Life of Brother André,* p. 44.

8.   Dubuc, p. 53.

9.   Quoted in Dubuc, p. 57.

10. Quoted in Ruffin, *Life of Brother André,* p. 55.

11. Quoted in Ruffin, *Life of Brother André,* pp. 45–46.

12. Quoted in Ruffin, *Life of Brother André,* p. 60.

13. Dubuc, p. 58.

14. Quoted in Ruffin, *Life of Brother André,* p. 137.

15. Quoted in Daniel F. McSheffery, "Brother André: Montréal's Miracle Man," www.catholic.net.

16. Quoted in Dubuc, p. 195.

17. Vanier, "Brother André," p. 9.

18. Story told by Lucie Drolet of her own healing as recounted in Ruffin, *Life of Brother André,* pp. 94–95.

19. Pichette, p. 32.

20. Quoted in Ruffin, *Life of Brother André,* p. 89.

Chapter Five: "Thank God Ahead of Time"

1.   Quoted in Crosby, *Solanus Casey,* p. 55.

2.   Quoted in Crosby, *Thank God,* pp. 180–181.

3.   Quoted in Crosby, *Thank God,* p. 118.

4.   Quoted in Ruffin, *Padre Pio,* p. 268.

5.   Quoted in Crosby, *Solanus Casey,* p. 56.

6.   Quoted in Catherine M. Odell, *Father Solanus: The Story of Solanus Casey, O.F.M. Cap. Updated* (Huntington, Ind.: Our Sunday Visitor, 1995), p. 69.

7.   Quoted in Crosby, *Solanus Casey,* p. 86.

8.   Wollenweber, p. 50.

9.   Quoted in Crosby, *Thank God,* p. 288.

10. Crosby, *Solanus Casey,* p. 71.

11. Crosby, *Solanus Casey,* p. 72.

12. Quoted in Crosby, *Solanus Casey,* p. 118.

13. Crosby, *Solanus Casey,* p. 86.

14. Quoted in Crosby, *Solanus Casey,* pp. 88–89.

15. Wollenweber, p. 78.

16. Quoted in Crosby, *Thank God,* p. 137.

17. Crosby, *Solanus Casey,* p. 29.

18. Quoted in Wollenweber, p. 76.

19. Quoted in Crosby, *Solanus Casey,* p. 236.

20. Quoted in Crosby, *Solanus Casey,* p. 262.

21. Quoted in Crosby, *Solanus Casey,* p. 157.

22. Quoted in Crosby, *Solanus Casey,* p. 101.

23. Crosby, *Solanus Casey,* p. 100.

Chapter Six: A Holy and Living Sacrifice

1. St. Albans, p. 6.

2. Quoted in Allegri, p. 137.

3. American Capuchin priest Father Joseph of the Italian Friary of Santa Maria delle Grazie, as quoted in St. Albans, p. 5.

4. Quoted in Allegri, p. 74.

5. Quoted in Allegri, p. 74.

6. Quoted in Allegri, pp. 71–72.

7. McCaffery, p. 83.

8. Quoted in Tangari, ix.

9. McCaffery, pp. 83–84.

10. McCaffery, p. 73.

11. McCaffery, p. 86.

12. Quoted in St. Albans, p. 93.

13. Quoted in St. Albans, p. 191.

14. McCaffery, p. 210.

15. McCaffery, p. 86.

16. McCaffery, p. 86.

17. McCaffery, p. 87.

18. Quoted in Ruffin, *Padre Pio,* pp. 294, 296.

19. McCaffery, p. 88.

20. Tangari, p. 50.

21. McCaffery, p. 96.

22. McCaffery, p. 96.

23. Tangari, p. 51.

24. Quoted in Tangari, p. 56.

25. McCaffery, p. 144.

26. Quoted in McCaffery, p. 156.

27. Quoted in McCaffery, pp. 98–99.

28. Quoted in Allegri, p. 6.

29. Giuseppe Canaponi, Tuscan railway worker, quoted in Allegri, p. 209.

30. Quoted in Allegri, p. 203.

31. Tangari, p. 51.

32. Tangari, p. 51.

33. St. Albans, p. 115.

34. McCaffery, p. 96.

35. Quoted in McCaffery, pp. 111–112.

36. McCaffery, p. 211.

37. Tangari, p. 49.

38. Quoted in McCaffery, p. 101.

39. McCaffery, p. 47.

40. McCaffery, pp. 48–50.

41. Quoted in Ruffin, *Life of Brother André*, p. 140.

42. Quoted in Wollenweber, p. 60.

43. Quoted in Crosby, *Solanus Casey*, p. 85.

44. Quoted in Ruffin, *Life of Brother André*, p. 7.

45. McCaffery, p. 20.

Chapter Seven: Healing Faith

1. Pichette, p. 35.

2. Quoted in Ruffin, *Life of Brother André*, p. 173.

3. Quoted in Ruffin, *Life of Brother André*, p. 90.

4. Quoted in Ruffin, *Life of Brother André*, p. 150.

5.   Quoted in Ruffin, *Life of Brother André,* p. 151.

6.   Crosby, *Solanus Casey,* p. 122.

7.   Quoted in Crosby, *Thank God,* p. 206.

8.   Quoted in Crosby, *Solanus Casey,* p. 159.

9.   Quoted in Crosby, *Solanus Casey,* p. 159.

10. Quoted in Wollenweber, p. 100.

11. Crosby, *Solanus Casey,* p. 243.

12. Quoted in Crosby, *Solanus Casey,* p. 165.

13. Quoted in Crosby, *Solanus Casey,* p. 160.

14. Quoted in Quoted in St. Albans, p. 171.

15. Quoted in St. Albans, p. 182.

16. Tangari, p. 69.

Part Three: HOLY WORKS

Chapter Eight: Works of Mercy

1.   Dubuc, p. 65.

2.   Pichette, pp. 28, 53.

3.   Quoted in Isabelle Bourbon, "Joseph Olivier Pichette," *The Oratory,* vol. 79, no. 2 (March–April 2005), p. 23.

4.   McCaffery, p. 217.

5.   McCaffery, p. 217.

6.   Allegri, p. 6.

7.   McCaffery, p. 155.

8.   Quoted in Crosby, *Solanus Casey,* p. 226.

9.   Quoted in Crosby, *Solanus Casey,* p. 216.

10. Quoted in Crosby, *Solanus Casey,* p. 198.

11. Quoted in Crosby, *Solanus Casey,* p. 93.

12. Quoted in Crosby, *Thank God,* p. 132.

13. Ruffin, *Life of Brother André,* p. 184.

14. Ruffin, *Padre Pio,* p. 272.

15. Ruffin, *Padre Pio,* p. 184.

16. McCaffery, p. 76.

17. Quoted in Ruffin, *Padre Pio,* p. 281.

18. Quoted in Ruffin, *Padre Pio,* p. 286.

19. *New York Times,* as quoted in Ruffin, *Padre Pio,* p. 286.

20. Quoted in Ruffin, *Padre Pio,* p. 287.

21. St. Albans, p. 145.

Chapter Nine: The Oratory of Saint Joseph

1. Quoted in Dubuc, p. 67.

2. Quoted in Ruffin, *Life of Brother André,* p. 51.

3. Quoted in Ruffin, *Life of Brother André,* p. 63.

4. Quoted in Dubuc, p. 207.

5. Dubuc, pp. 68–69.

6. Quoted in Dubuc, p. 69.

7. From the *Annals of Saint Joseph,* as quoted in "Brothers Aldéric and Abundius," in *The Oratory,* vol. 78, no. 1 (January–February 2004), p. 13.

8. Article in *La Presse,* Montréal, October 7, 1904, as quoted in Dubuc, p. 70.

9. Archbishop Paul Bruschési, as quoted in Dubuc, pp. 176–177.

10. Dubuc, p. 174.

11. Quoted in Ruffin, *Life of Brother André,* p. 165.

12. Quoted in Ruffin, *Life of Brother André,* p. 168.

13. Quoted in Ruffin, *Life of Brother André,* p. 164.

14. Quoted in Dubuc, p. 233.

15. Dubuc, p. 205.

16. Father Jules Beaulac, letter on his Web site, quoted in Jean-Pierre Aumont, c.s.c., "Rector's Word," *The Oratory,* vol. 78, no. 1 (January–February 2004), p. 3.

17. Jean-Pierre Aumont, "Rector's Word," *The Oratory*, vol. 77, no. 5 (September–October 2003), p. 4.

18. Cardinal Jean-Claude Turcotte, "A House of Grace and Salvation," *The Oratory* 79 (January–February 2005), p. 11.

Part Four: HOLY LIVES

Chapter Ten: Rapt in Prayer

1. Quoted in Odell, pp. 178–179.

2. Crosby, *Thank God*, p. 271.

3. Account by biographer Leona Garrity, as quoted in Crosby, *Solanus Casey*, p. 128.

4. St. Albans, p. 80.

Chapter Eleven: Humility

1. Quoted in Pichette, p. 45.

2. Ruffin, *Life of Brother André*, p. 131.

3. Father Blase Gitzen, quoted in Odell, p. 169.

4. Quoted in Crosby, *Solanus Casey*, p. 245.

5. Quoted in Crosby, *Solanus Casey*, p. 245.

6. Quoted in Crosby, *Solanus Casey*, p. 243.

7. Ruffin, *Life of Brother André*, pp. 122–123.

8. Interview with Father André Léveillé, August 2003.

9. Pichette, p. 66.

10. Quoted in Dubuc, p. 231.

11. Quoted in Ruffin, *Life of Brother André*, p. 45.

12. Quoted in Ruffin, *Life of Brother André*, p. 61.

13. Ruffin, *Life of Brother André*, p. 89.

14. Quoted in McCaffery, pp. 110–111.

15. Quoted in Ruffin, *Padre Pio*, p. 373.

16. Quoted in Ruffin, *Padre Pio*, p. 303.

17. Quoted in St. Albans, p. 61.

Chapter Twelve: Grace in Suffering

1.   McCaffery, p. 217.
2.   Quoted in Ruffin, *Life of Brother André*, p. 7.
3.   Quoted in Ruffin, *Life of Brother André*, p. 149.
4.   Allegri, p. 87.
5.   Quoted in Allegri, p. 98.
6.   Quoted in Allegri, p. 100.
7.   Quoted in Ruffin, *Padre Pio*, p. 197.
8.   Quoted in Ruffin, *Padre Pio*, p. 196.
9.   McCaffery, p. 173.
10. Quoted in Ruffin, *Padre Pio*, p. 293.
11. McCaffery, p. 127, emphasis added.
12. Quoted in Ruffin, *Padre Pio*, p. 353.
13. Quoted in Ruffin, *Life of Brother André*, p. 161.
14. Quoted in McCaffery, p. 192.
15. Quoted in Ruffin, *Life of Brother André*, p. 126.
16. Quoted in Ruffin, *Life of Brother André*, pp. 126–127.
17. Quoted in Crosby, *Thank God*, p. 112.

Chapter Thirteen: Holy Deaths

1.   Quoted in Ruffin, *Life of Brother André*, p. 126.
2.   Quoted in Ruffin, *Life of Brother André*, p. 126.
3.   Quoted in Dubuc, p. 16.
4.   Quoted in Ruffin, *Life of Brother André*, p. 125.
5.   Ruffin, *Life of Brother André*, p. 126.
6.   Ruffin, *Life of Brother André*, p. 186.
7.   Quoted in Ruffin, *Life of Brother André*, p. 187.
8.   Quoted in Ruffin, *Life of Brother André*, p. 188.
9.   Quoted in Ruffin, *Life of Brother André*, p. 191.
10. Quoted in Ruffin, *Life of Brother André*, p. 191.
11. Quoted in Ruffin, *Life of Brother André*, p. 193.
12. Quoted in Ruffin, *Life of Brother André*, p. 193.

13. Quoted in Ruffin, *Life of Brother André,* pp. 192–193.

14. Quoted in Ruffin, *Life of Brother André,* p. 193.

15. Quoted in Ruffin, *Padre Pio,* p. 77.

16. Quoted in Crosby, *Solanus Casey,* p. 101.

17. Quoted in Ruffin, *Life of Brother André,* p. 195.

18. Pichette, p. 77.

19. Quoted in Ruffin, *Life of Brother André,* p. 197.

20. Quoted in Ruffin, *Life of Brother André,* p. 198.

21. Pichette, p. 84.

22. Saint Francis of Assisi, "Canticle of the Sun," adapted from quote in Omer Englebert, *St. Francis of Assisi: A Biography* (Cincinnati: Servant, 1979), p. 268.

23. Quoted in Wollenweber, p. 105.

24. Quoted in Wollenweber, pp. 105–106.

25. Quoted in Odell, p. 190.

26. Quoted in Odell, p. 191.

27. Quoted in Crosby, *Solanus Casey,* p. 143.

28. Quoted in Crosby, *Thank God,* p. 244.

29. Quoted in Crosby, *Thank God,* p. 244.

30. Quoted in Crosby, *Solanus Casey,* p. 146.

31. Quoted in Crosby, *Thank God,* p. 244.

32. Quoted in Crosby, *Thank God,* p. 244.

33. Quoted in Crosby, *Thank God,* p. 245.

34. Quoted in Crosby, *Solanus Casey,* p. 150.

35. Letter of Capuchin minister general Father Benignus of Sant' Ilario, quoted in Wollenweber, p. 113.

36. Quoted in Ruffin, *Padre Pio,* p. 373.

37. Quoted in Ruffin, *Padre Pio,* p. 375.

38. Quoted in Ruffin, *Padre Pio,* p. 377.

39. Quoted in Allegri, p. 252.

40. Quoted in Ruffin, *Padre Pio,* p. 372.

41. Quoted in Ruffin, *Padre Pio,* p. 132.

42.   Ruffin, *Padre Pio,* p. 405.

43.   John S. Tieman, "Reflections of an Inner City Teacher," *The Oratory,* vol. 77, no. 5 (September–October 2003), pp. 14–15.

44.   Dubuc, pp. 235–237.

Printed in the United States
By Bookmasters